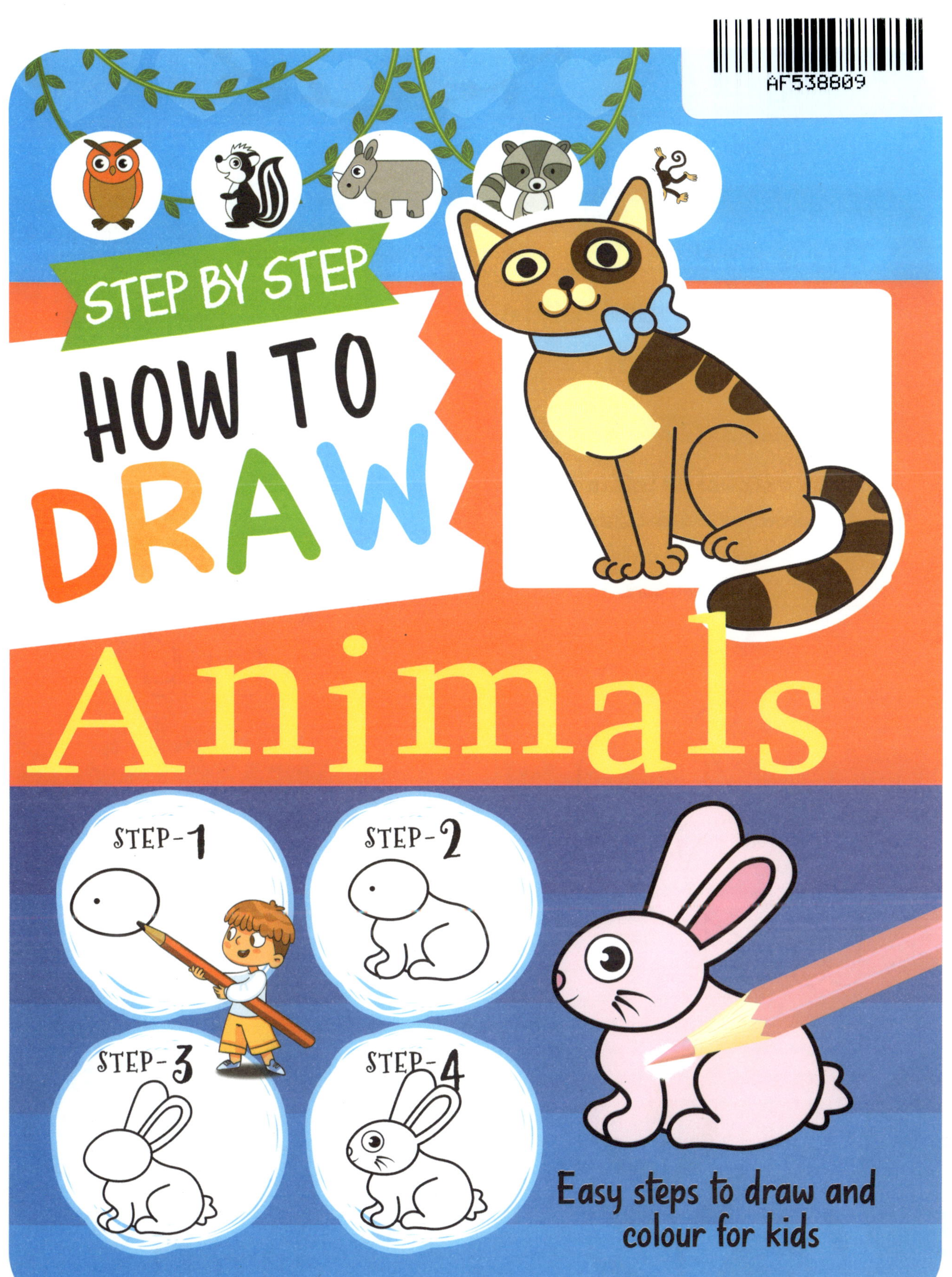

AF538809
STEP BY STEP
HOW TO
DRAW
Animals
STEP-1
STEP-2
STEP-3
STEP-4
Easy steps to draw and colour for kids

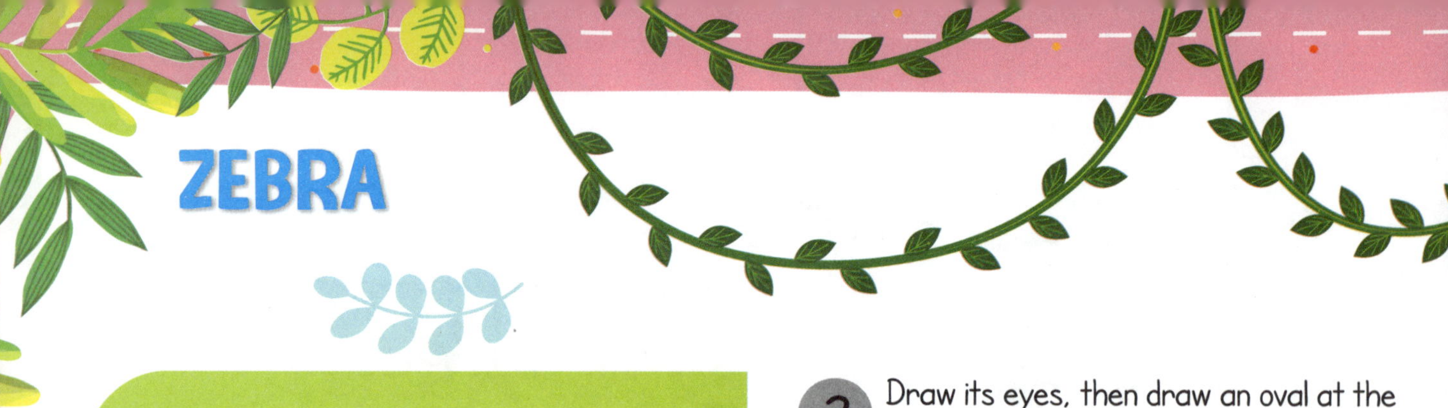

ZEBRA

This is a zebra. It has a brilliant black-and-white striped coat.

1 Draw a circle at the bottom of the page then draw four cylindrical shapes for legs. Draw a neck and an oval face then draw two ears.

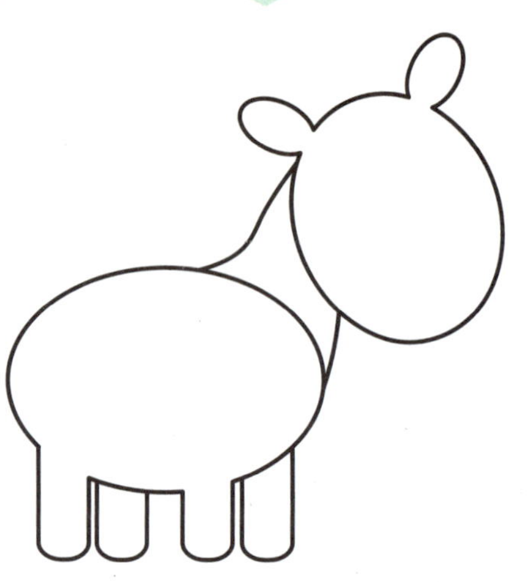

2 Draw its eyes, then draw an oval at the bottom of the face. Outline its mouth, tail and ears.

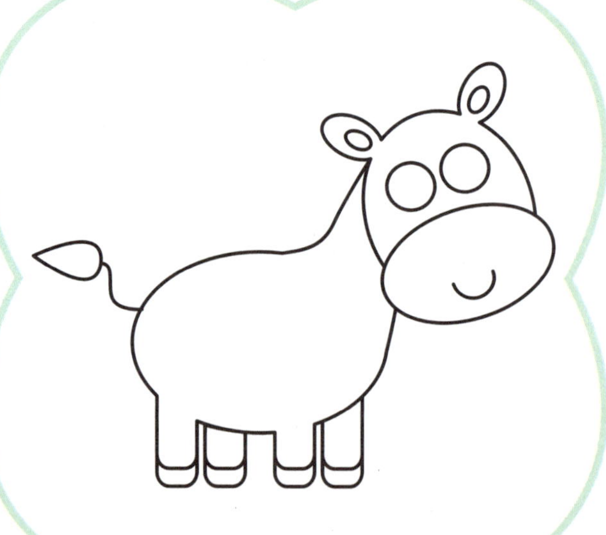

3 Draw its hair at the top of its head. Finish sketching its eyes and its nose.

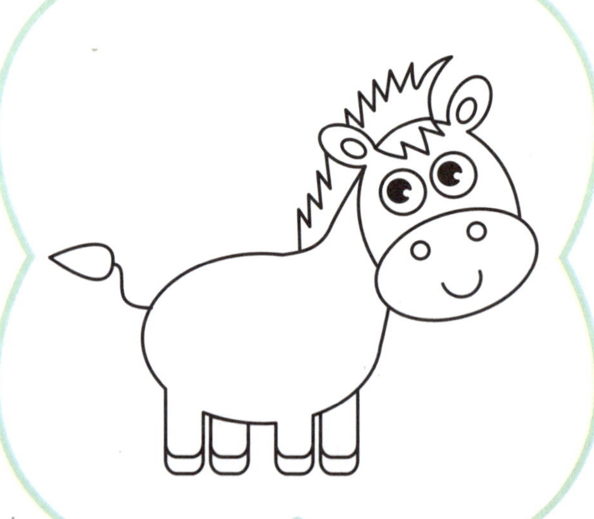

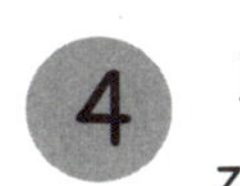

4 Draw beautiful stripes all over the zebra's body and fill them with black colour.

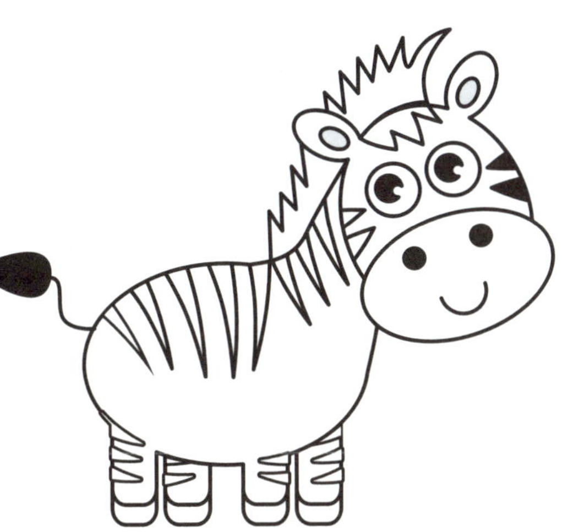

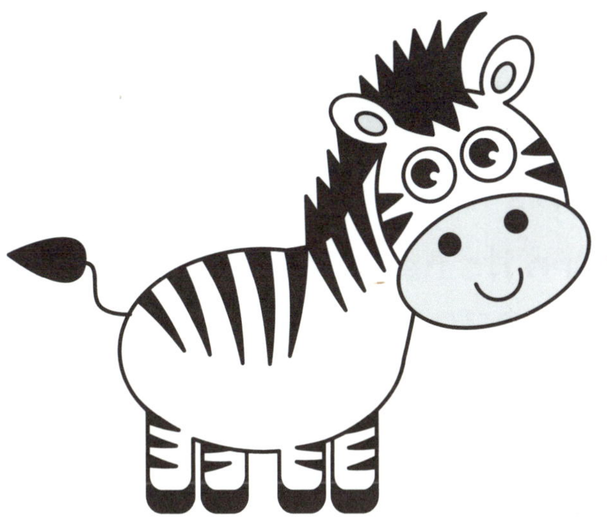

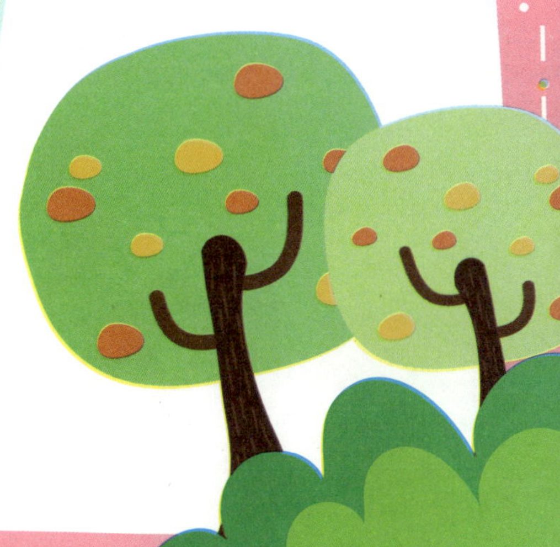

OWL

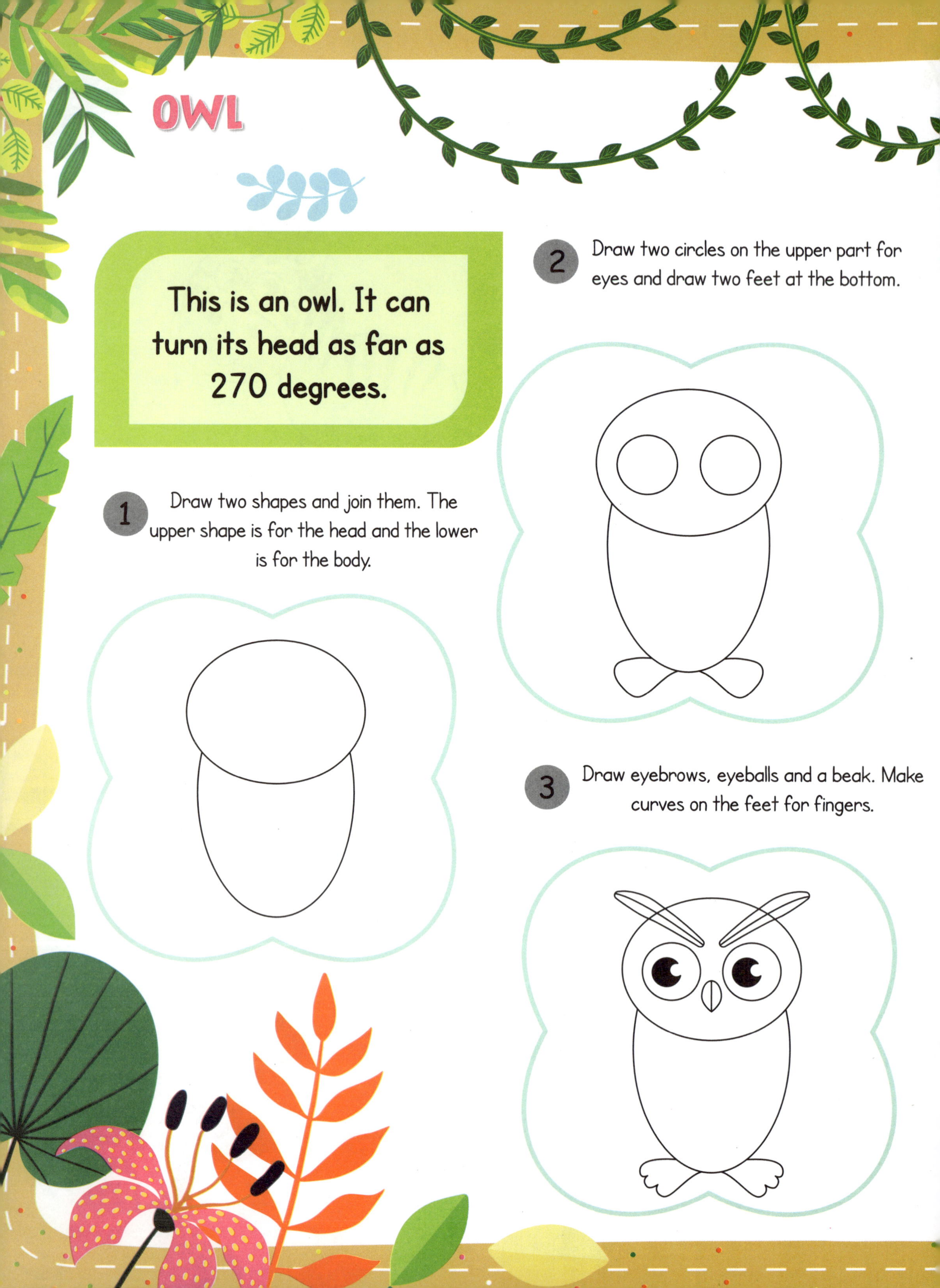

This is an owl. It can turn its head as far as 270 degrees.

1 Draw two shapes and join them. The upper shape is for the head and the lower is for the body.

2 Draw two circles on the upper part for eyes and draw two feet at the bottom.

3 Draw eyebrows, eyeballs and a beak. Make curves on the feet for fingers.

4 Draw wings and draw lines on the feet to define claws. Erase unwanted lines.

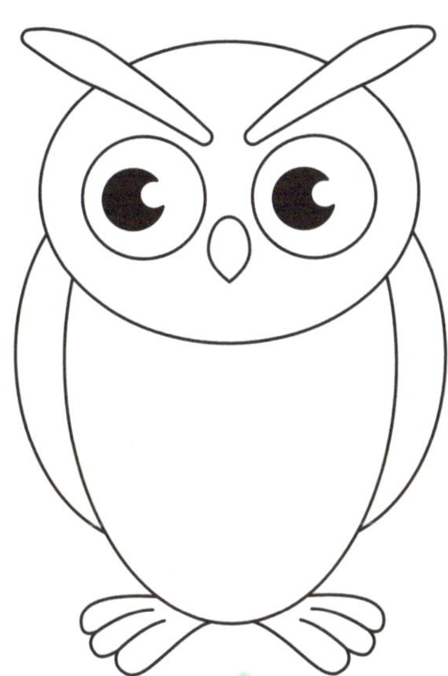

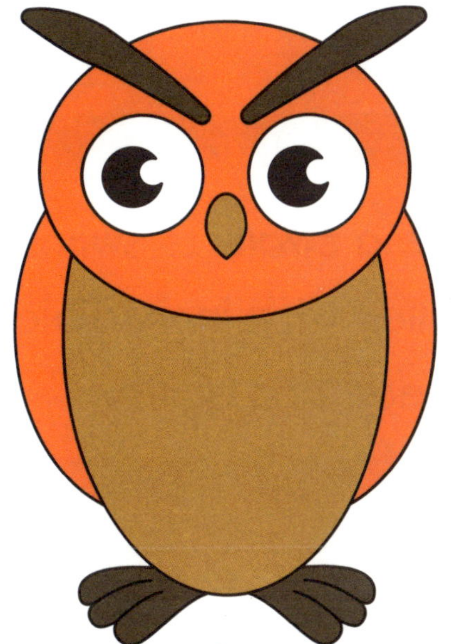

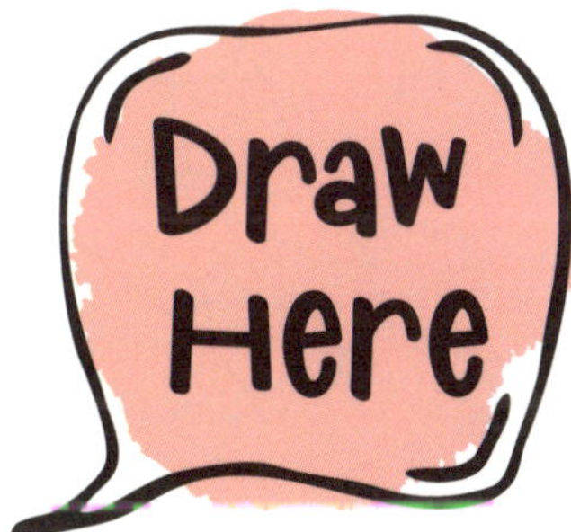

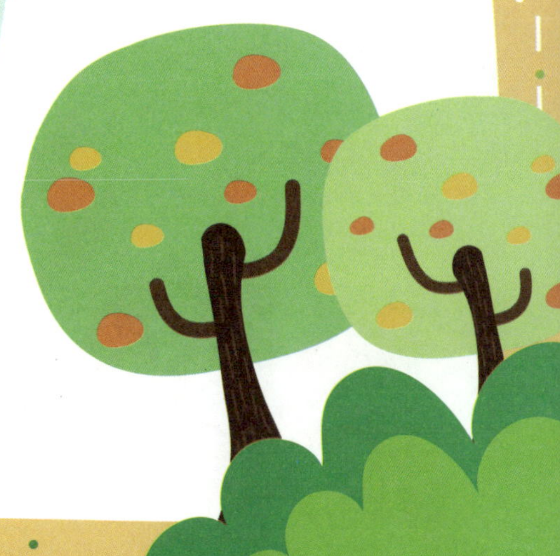

SWAN

This is a swan. It swims and flies with incredible speed and agility.

1 Draw an oval for the face and a triangular cone on it for the beak. Draw a long curve down for the neck.

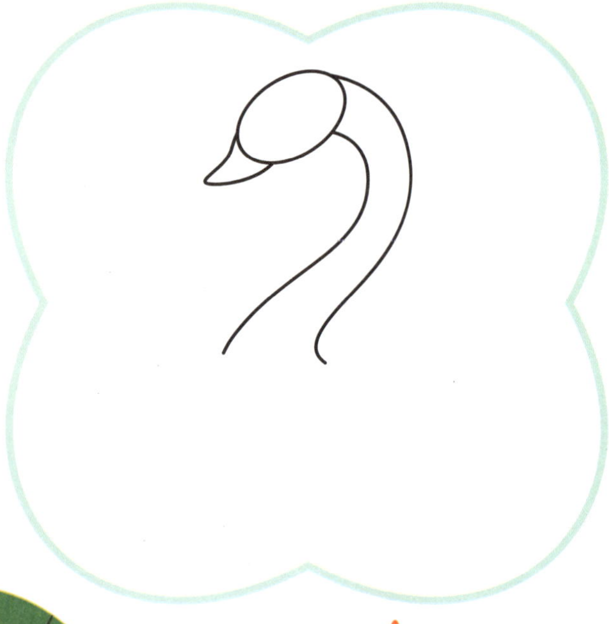

2 Below the neck, draw the shape of the body.

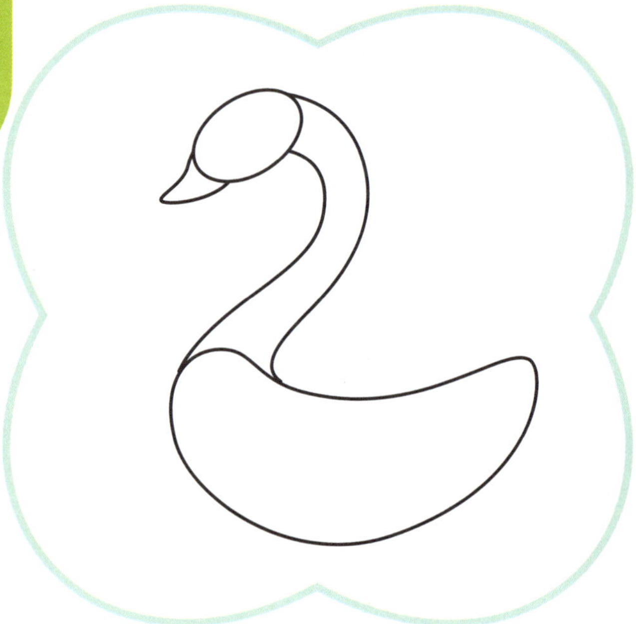

3 Make the letter W at the back end of the body.

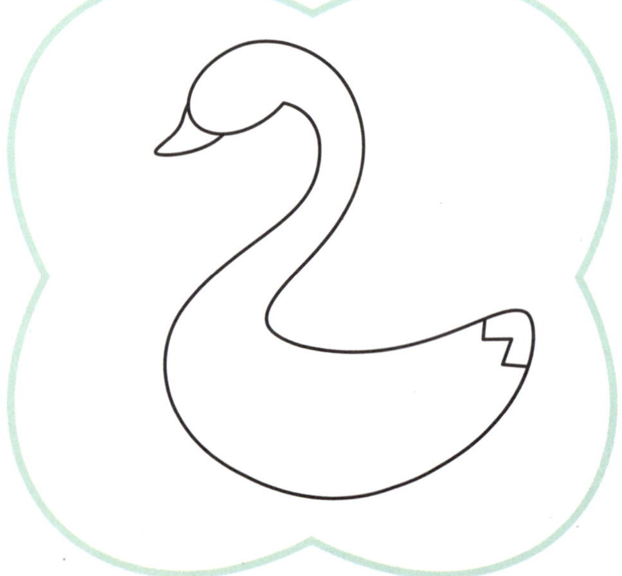

4 Make an eye and the eyeball and darken the area under the eye. Just at the end of the neck, draw the wing.

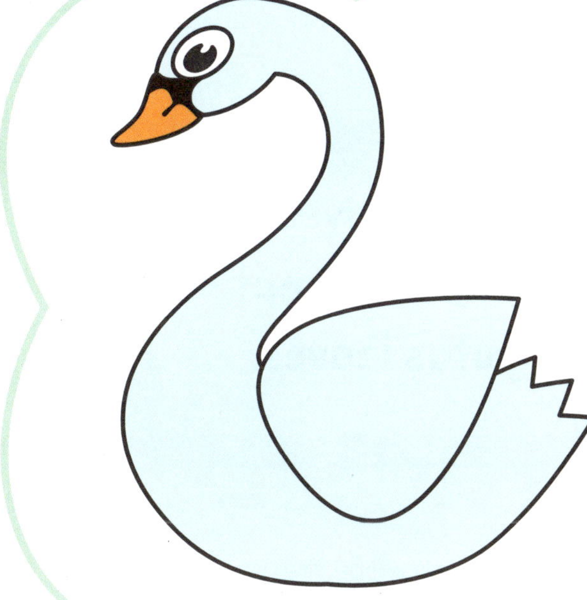

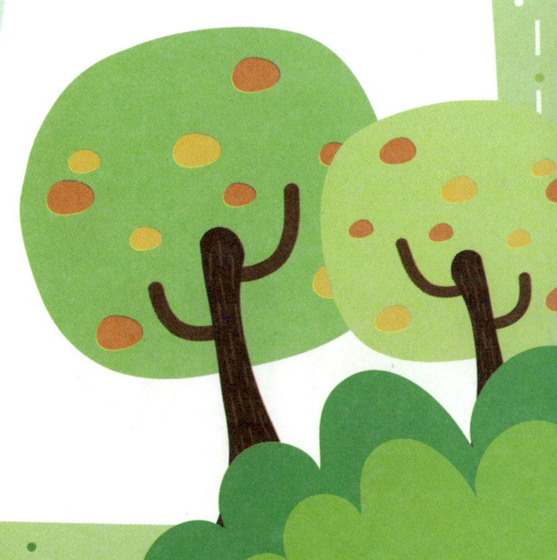

KOALA

Koalas are natives of Australia. They eat eucalyptus leaves.

1 Draw a circle which will be the face of the koala.

2 Draw its eyes and arms.

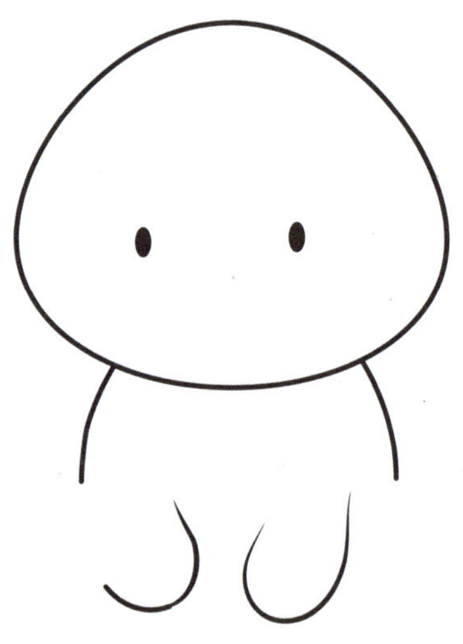

3 Draw the koala's body, legs and ears.

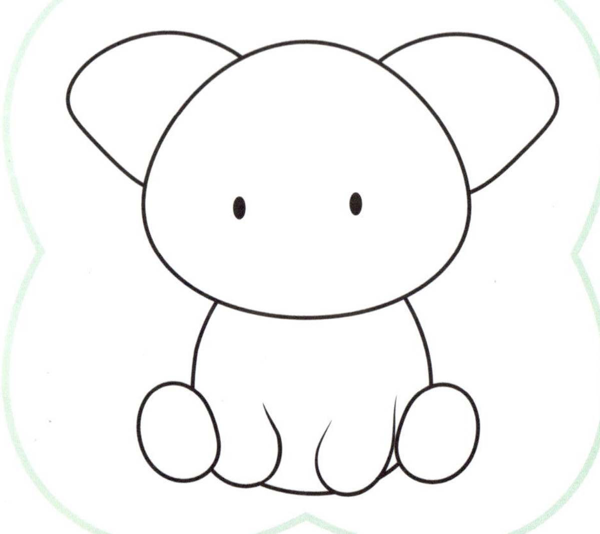

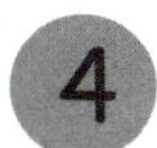

4 Draw its nose along with other details and colour it as shown.

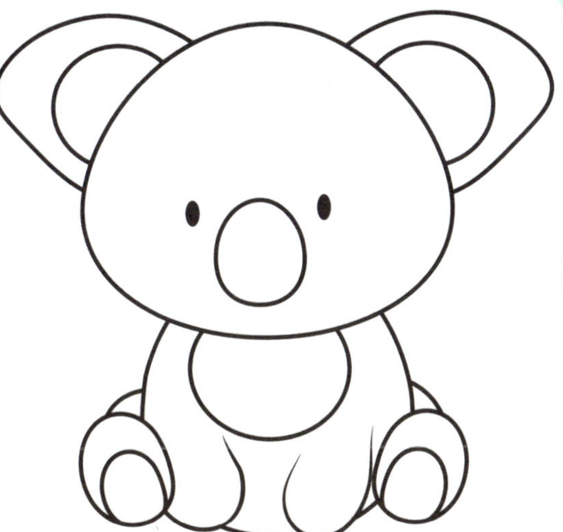

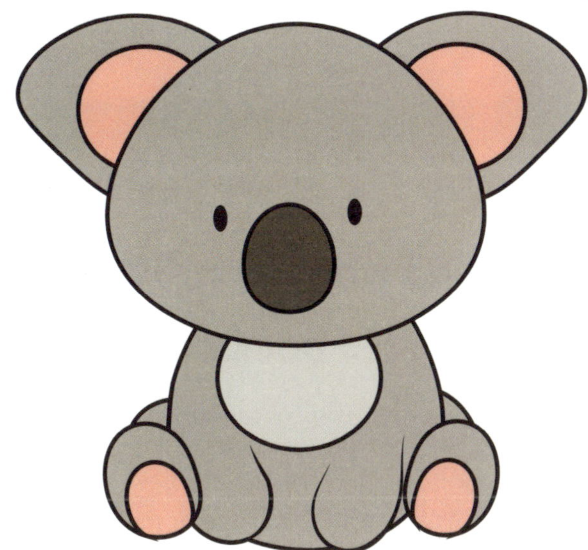

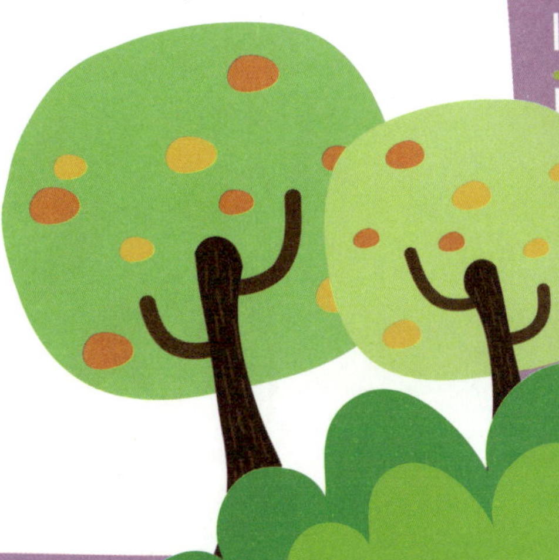

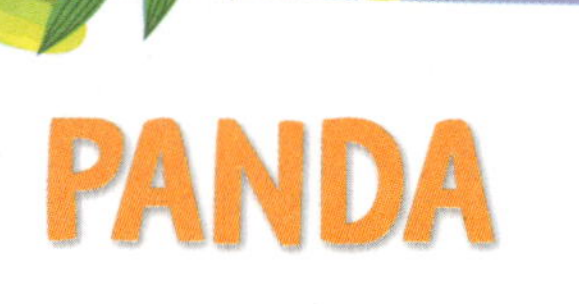

This is a panda. It has black and white fur. It mainly eats bamboo.

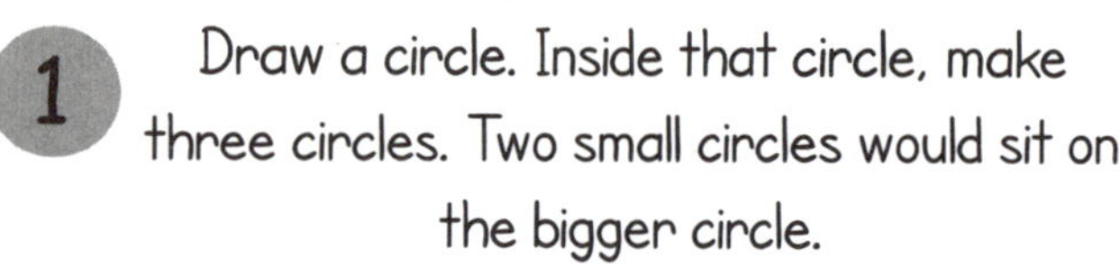

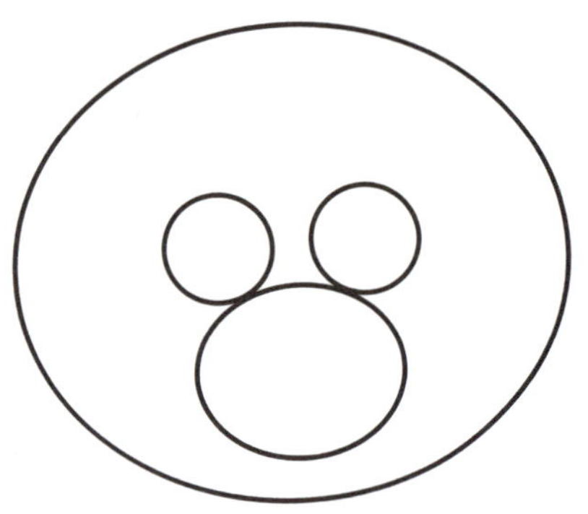

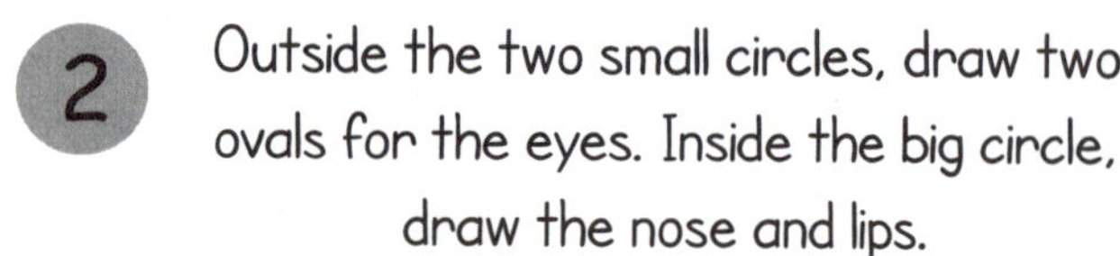

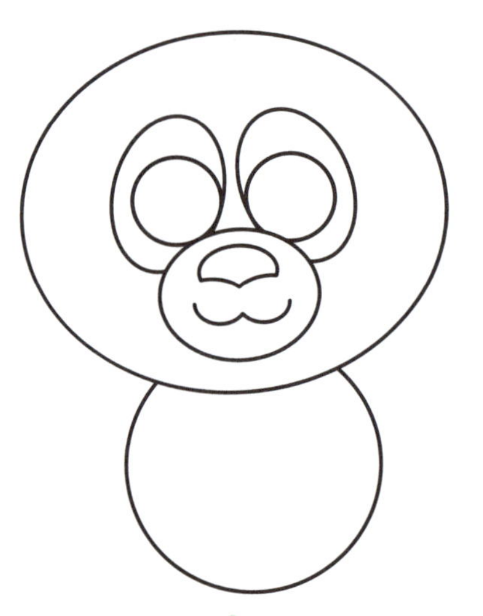

3 Draw semi-circles for ears and draw four limbs.

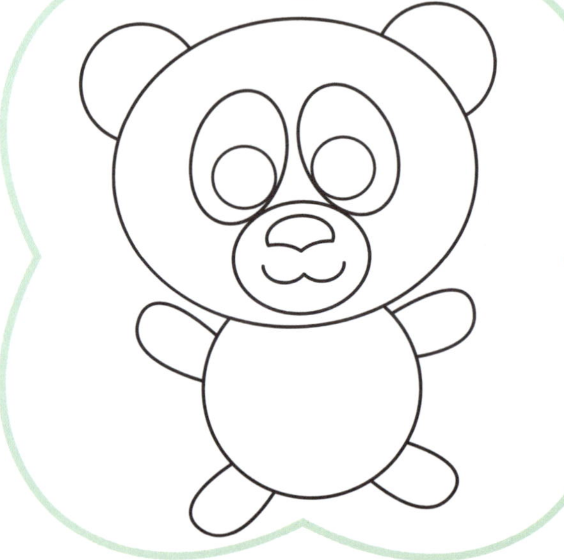

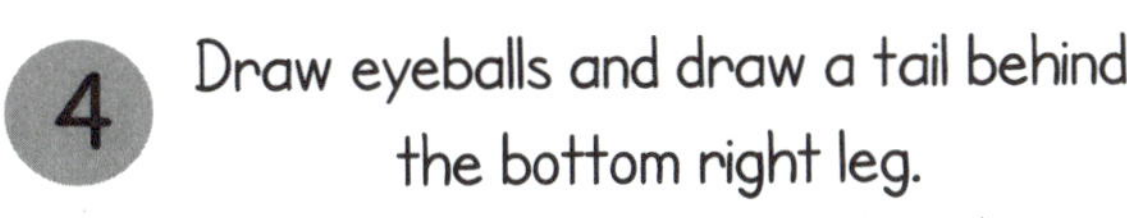

4 Draw eyeballs and draw a tail behind the bottom right leg.

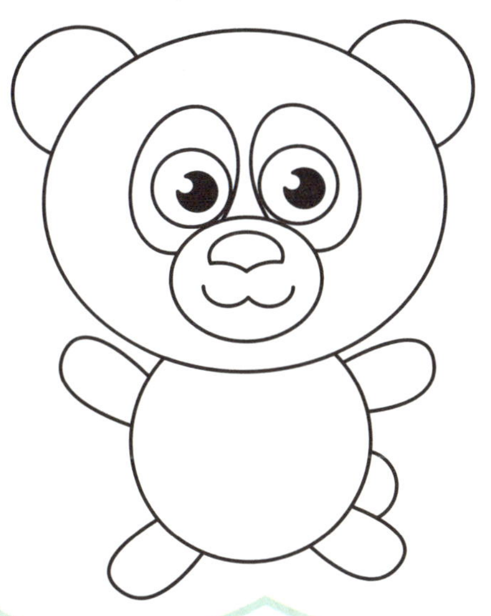

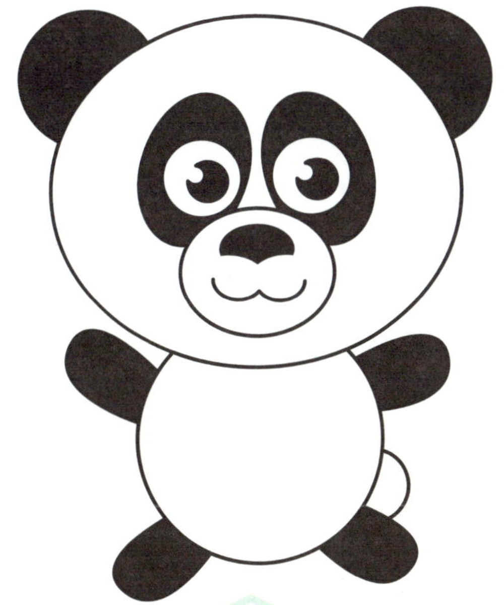

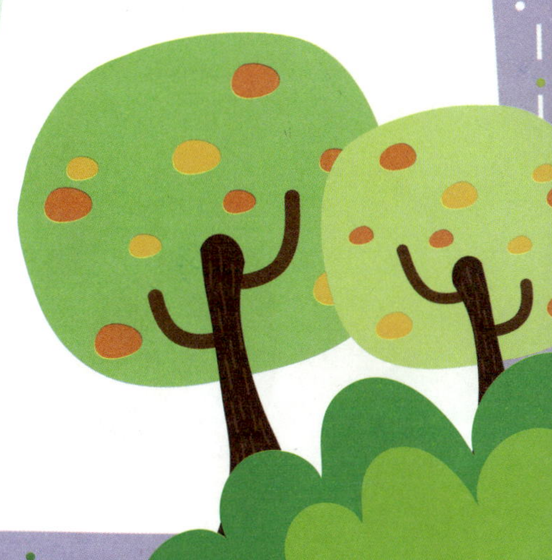

FROG

This is a frog. It has smooth, moist skin and big, bulging eyes.

1 Draw two circles for the face and body. Make curves on the upper circle for eyes.

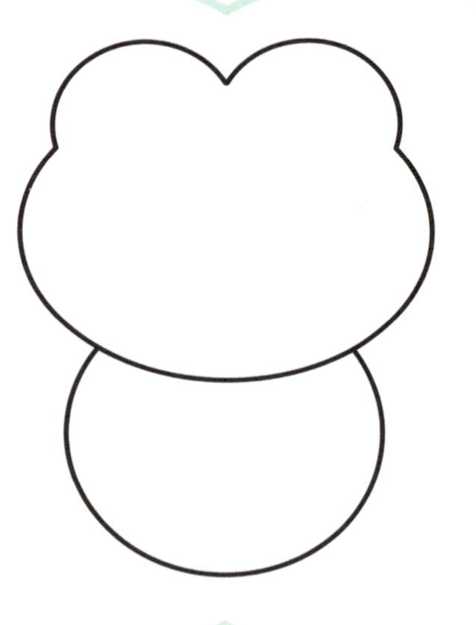

2 Draw a semi-circle inside the lower circle for the tummy and two ovals for legs.

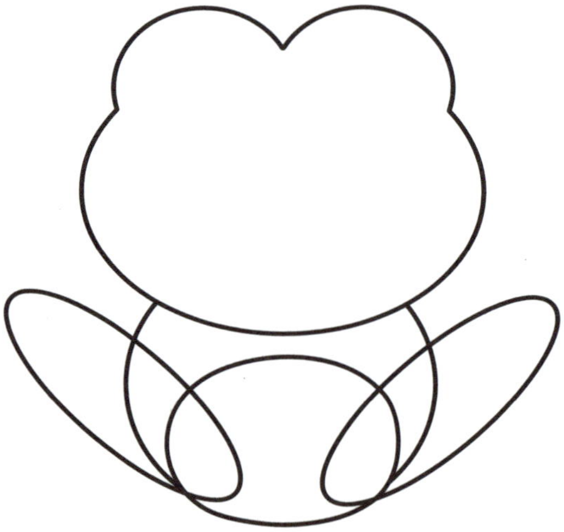

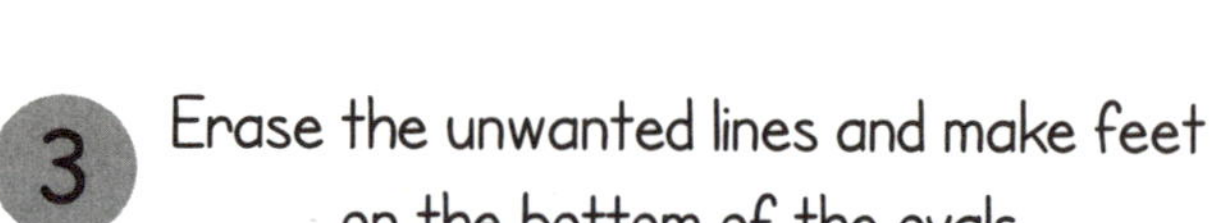

3 Erase the unwanted lines and make feet on the bottom of the ovals.

4 Draw the mouth, eyeballs, lines inside the legs and tiny circles at the ends of the feet.

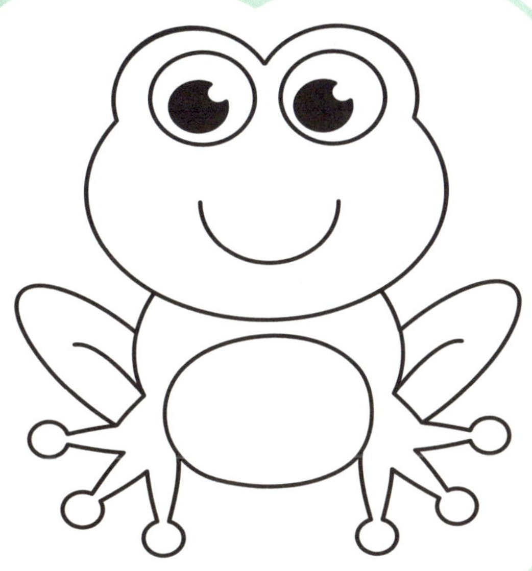

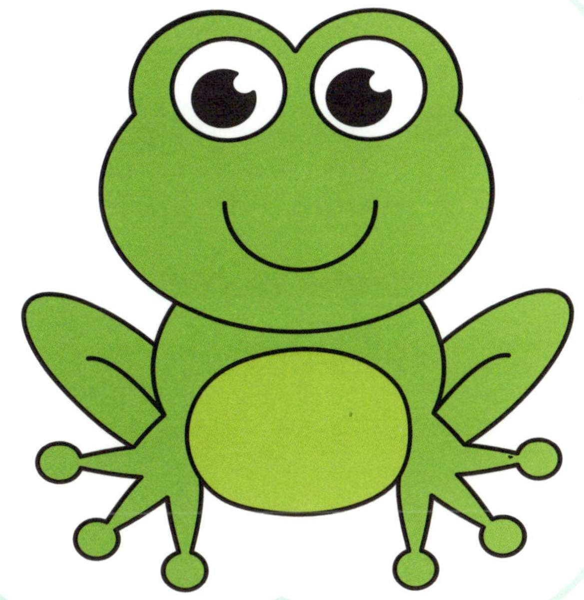

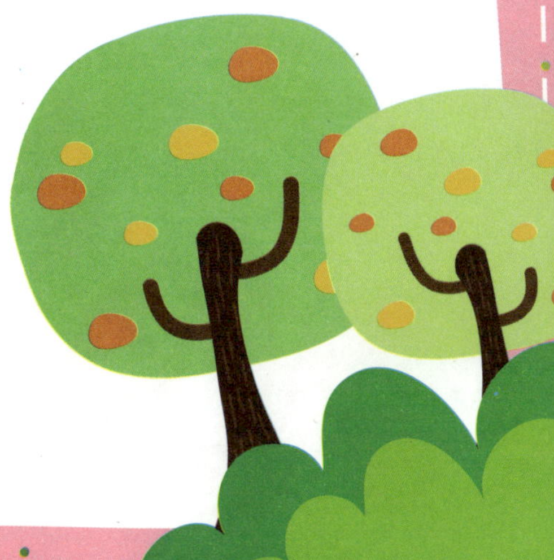

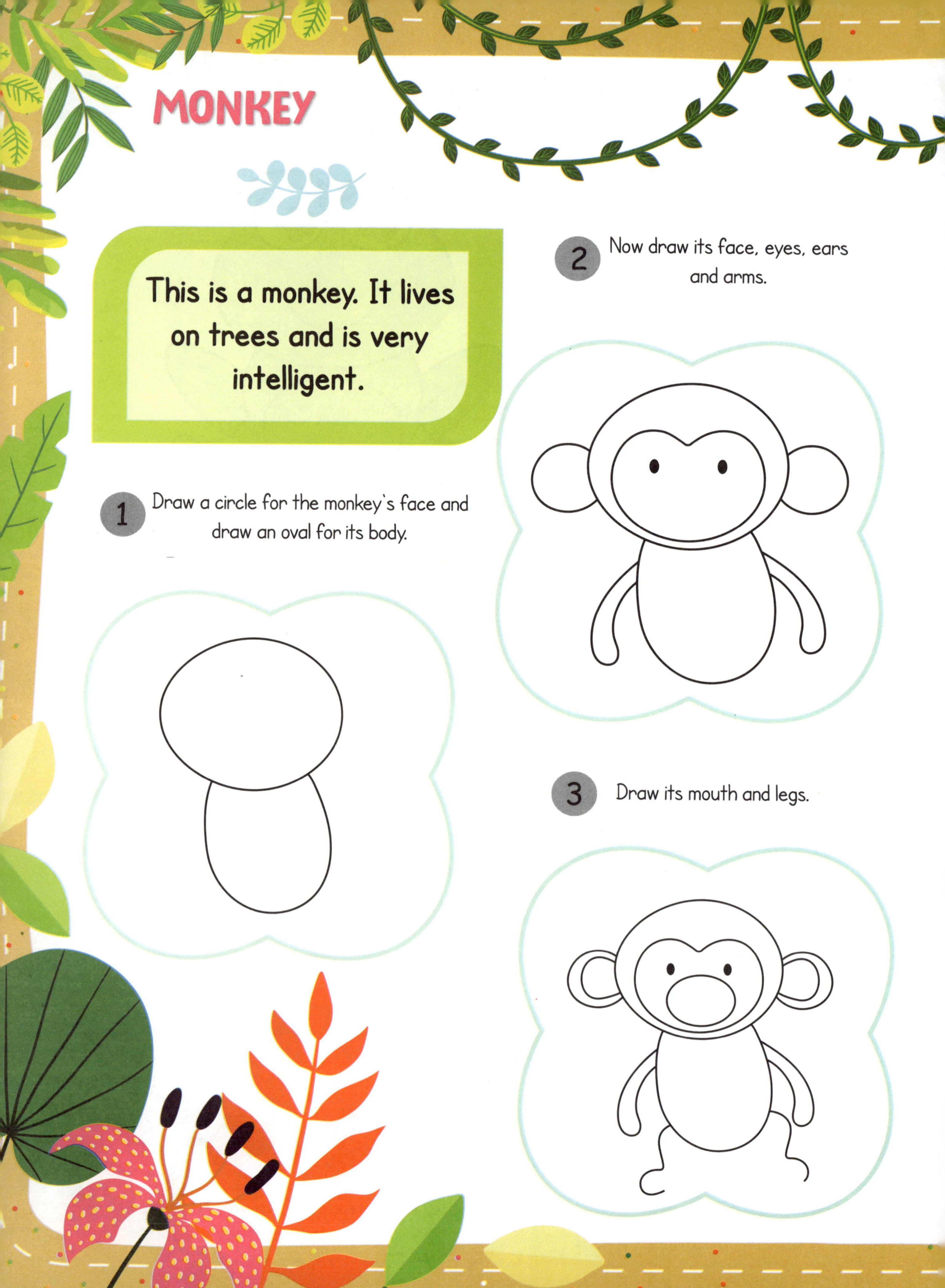

MONKEY

This is a monkey. It lives on trees and is very intelligent.

1 Draw a circle for the monkey's face and draw an oval for its body.

2 Now draw its face, eyes, ears and arms.

3 Draw its mouth and legs.

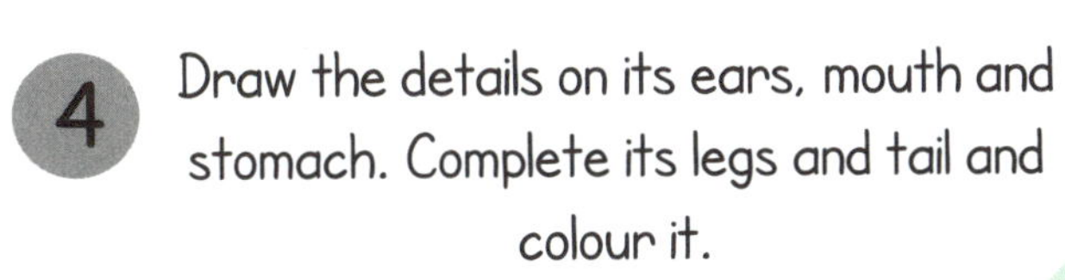

4 Draw the details on its ears, mouth and stomach. Complete its legs and tail and colour it.

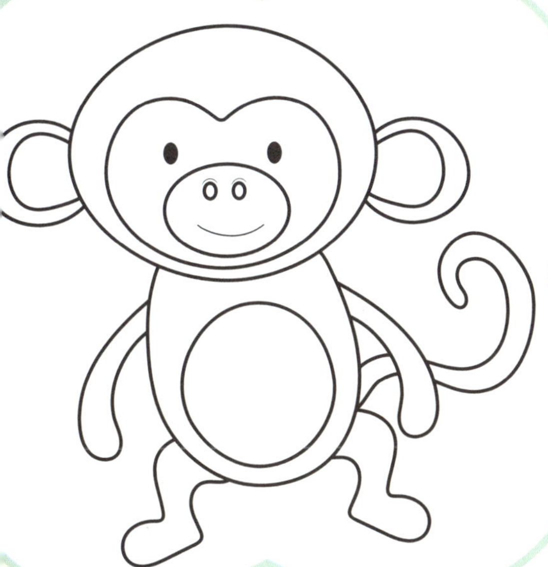

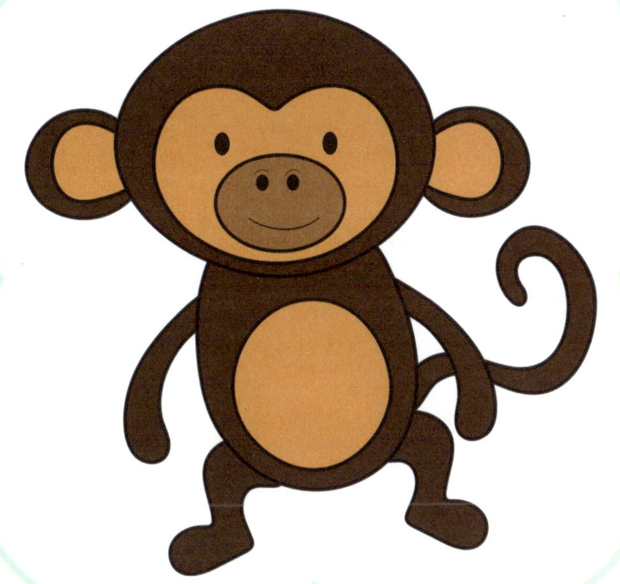

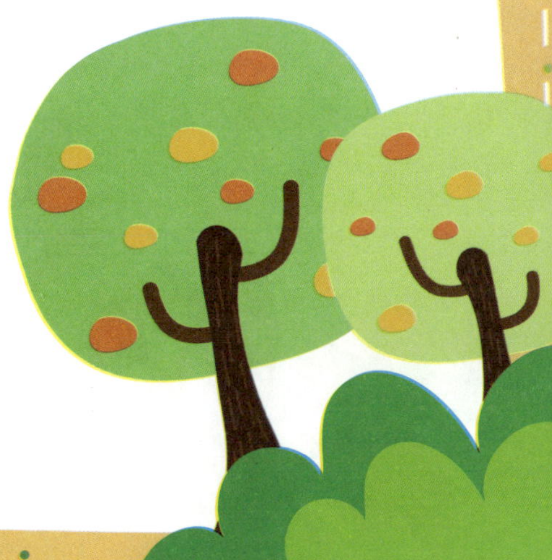

ALLIGATOR

This is an alligator. Its eyes glow in the dark.

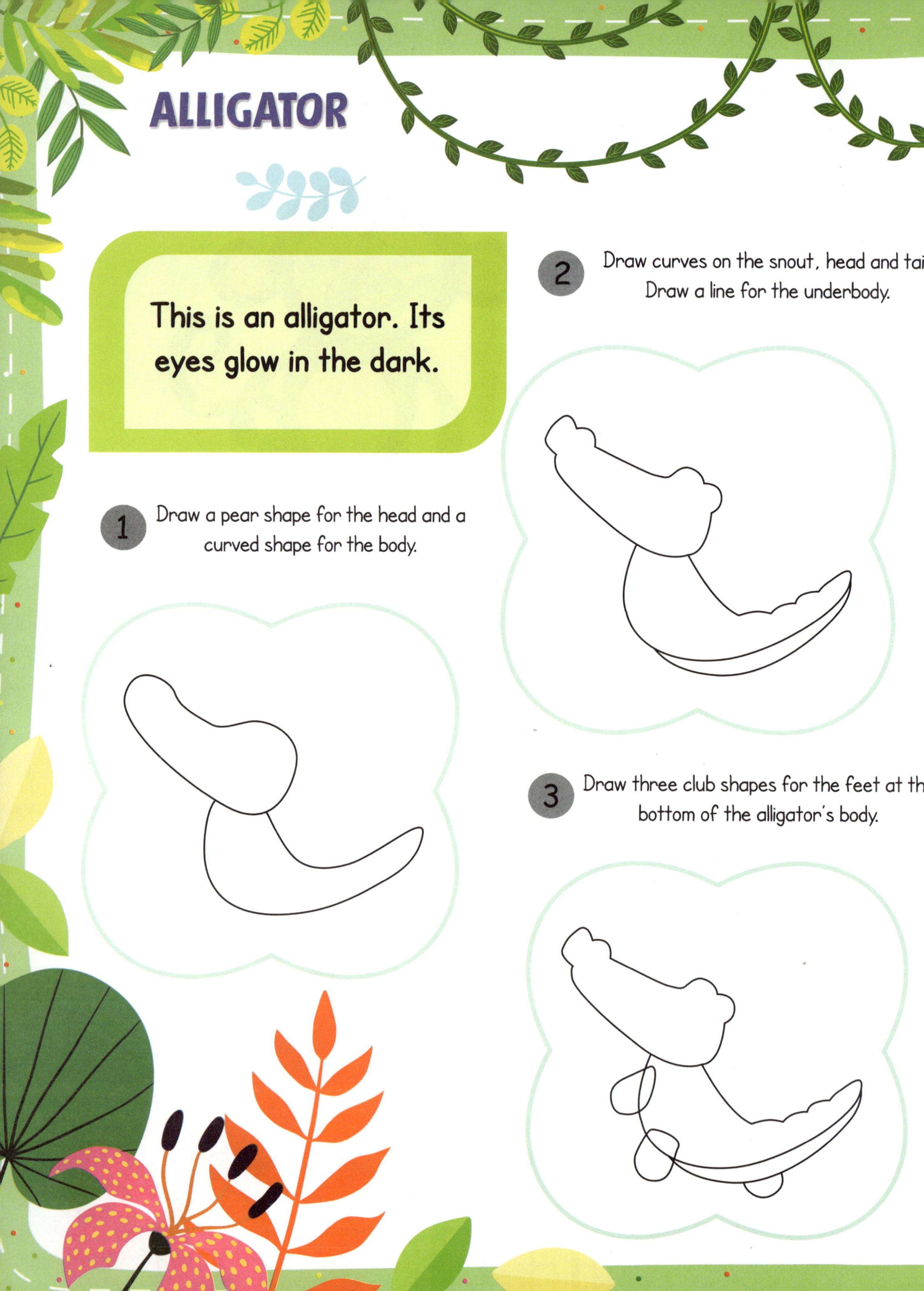

1 Draw a pear shape for the head and a curved shape for the body.

2 Draw curves on the snout, head and tail. Draw a line for the underbody.

3 Draw three club shapes for the feet at the bottom of the alligator's body.

4 Draw circles for the eyes and nostrils. Draw a line on the face for the mouth. Also, make two tiny V-shapes for teeth.

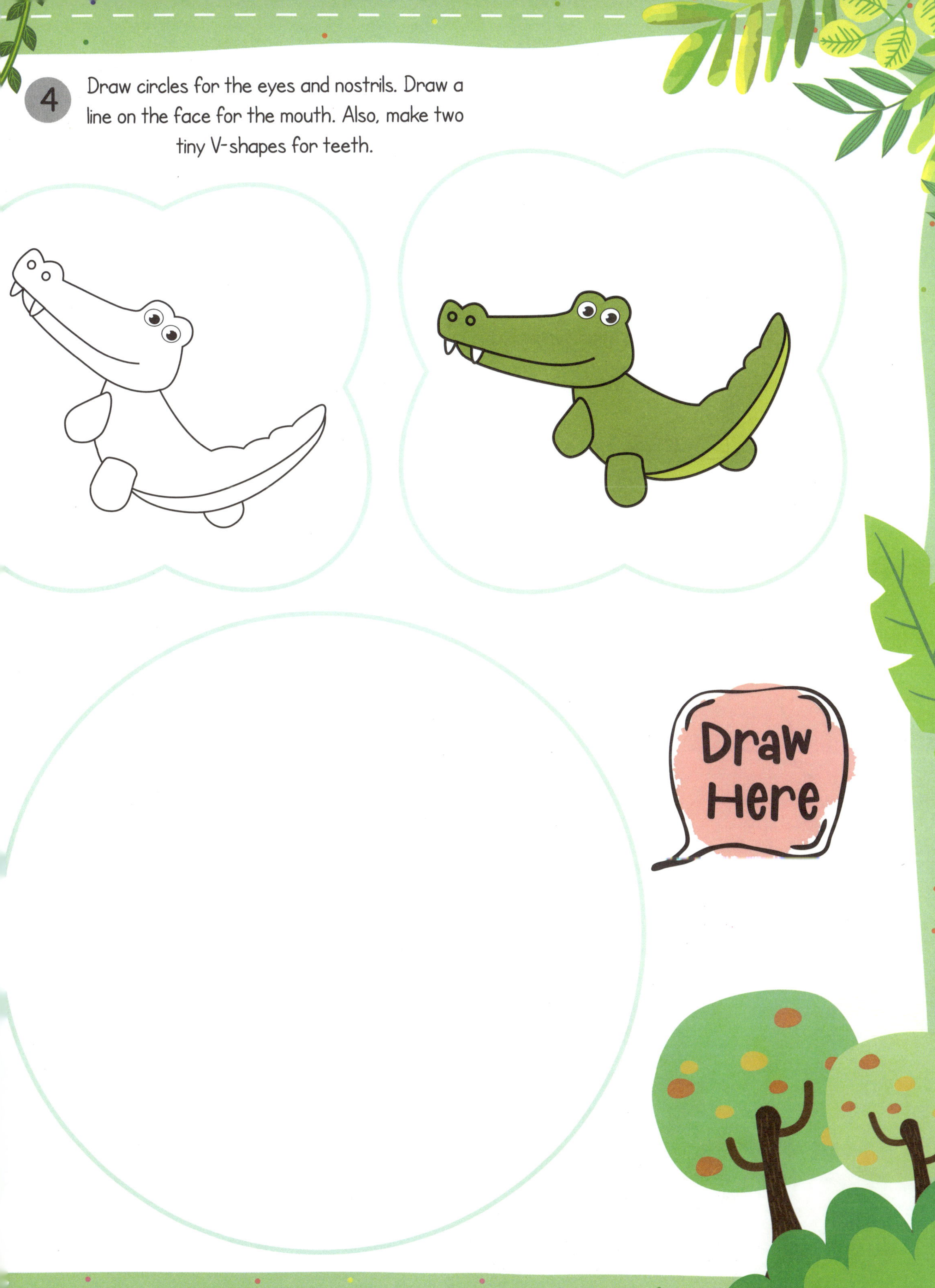

HIPPOPOTAMUS

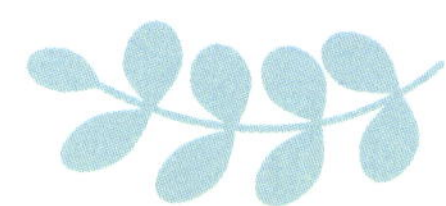

This is a hippopotamus. It's the third largest mammal on Earth.

1 Draw an oval shape and below it, draw a half-oval shape. At the top, make a circle, then rub it to draw two ears.

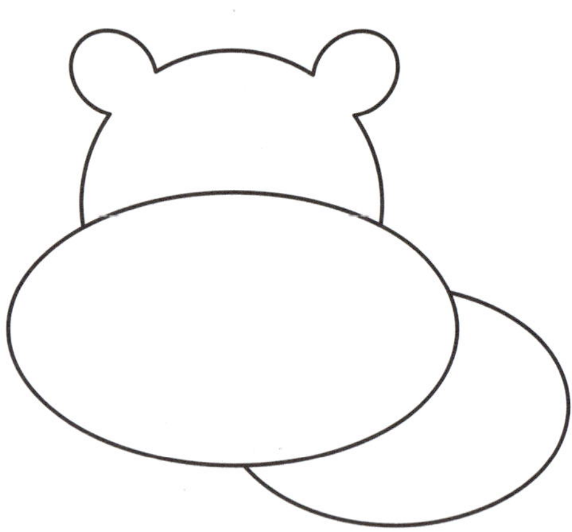

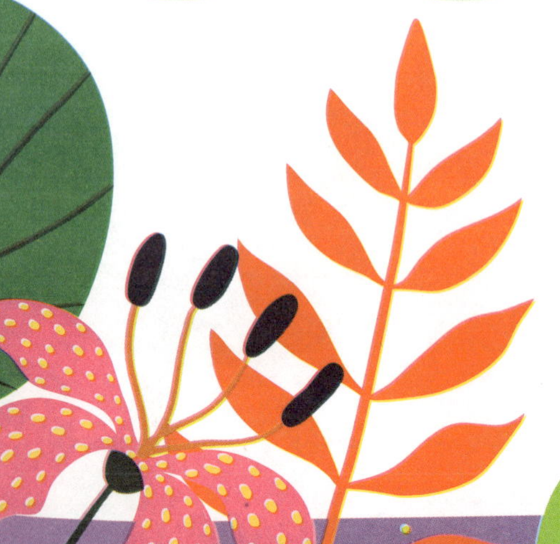

2 Use an eraser and pencil to draw legs on the half-oval.

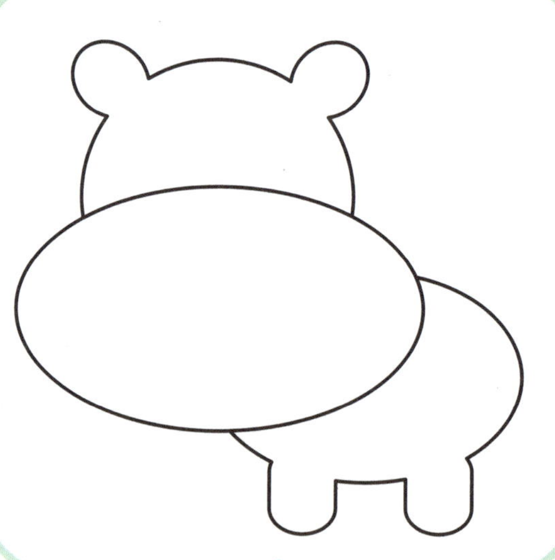

3 Inside the big oval, draw two equidistant small circles to make nostrils.

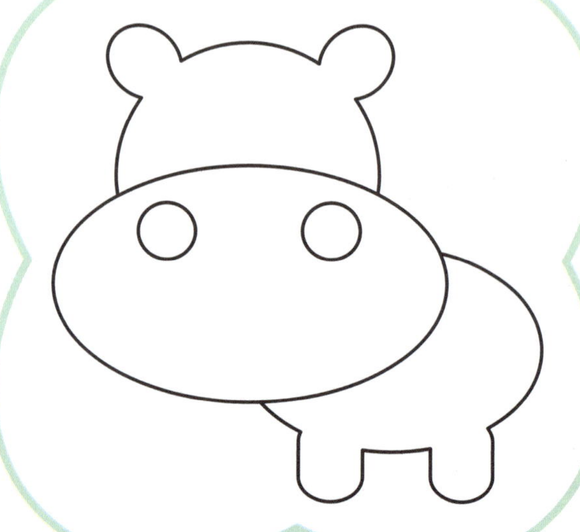

4 Draw two small circles for eyes and make pupils.
Draw a mouth and two teeth below the nostrils.
Draw a tiny tail.

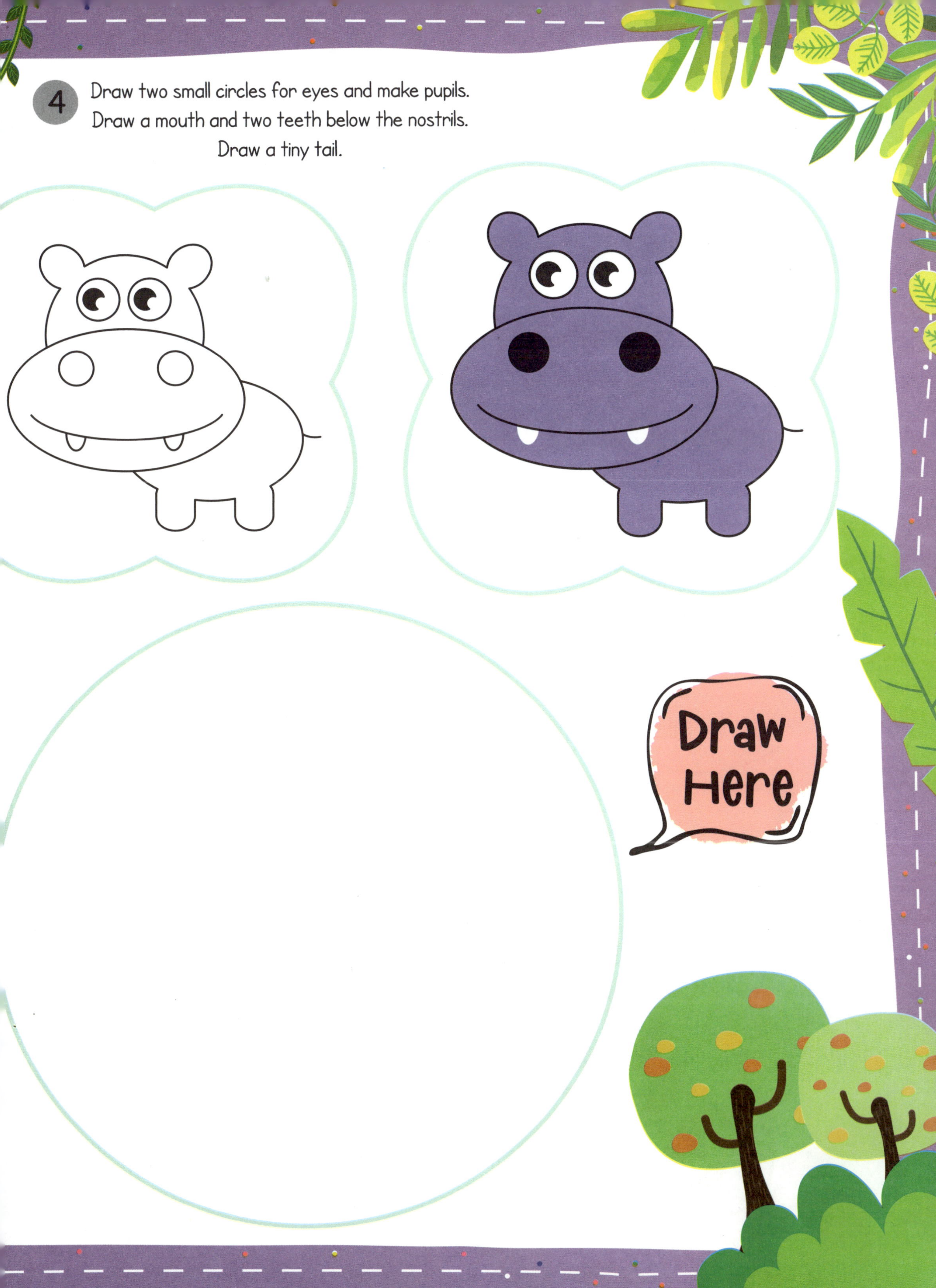

FLAMINGO

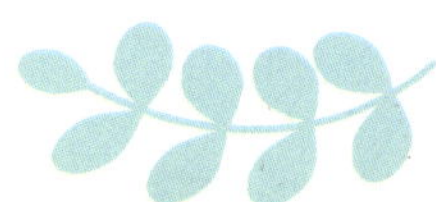

This is a flamingo. They are long-legged birds that are covered in bright pink feathers.

1 Draw a droplet shape on the paper.

2 Draw its neck and draw an oval for its face.

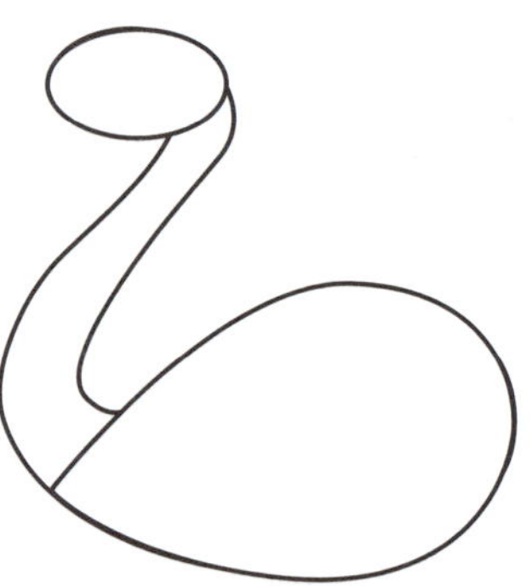

3 Draw its beak, feathers and tail.

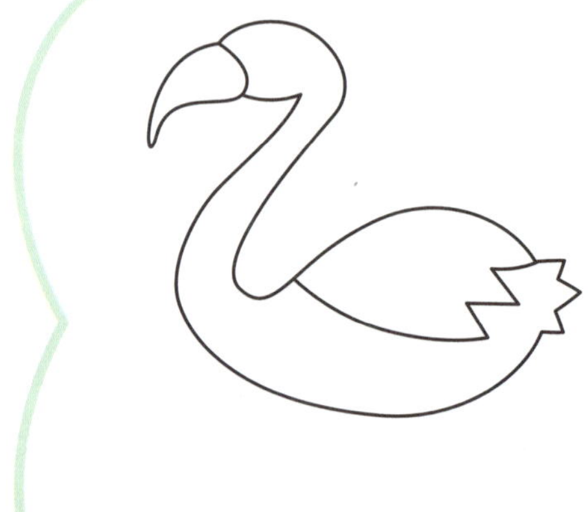

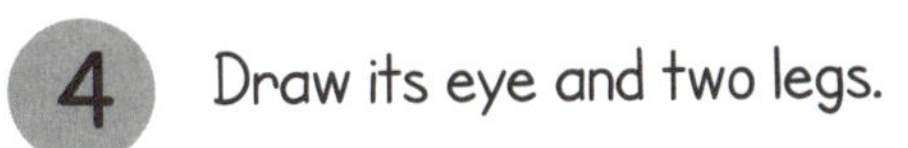

4 Draw its eye and two legs.

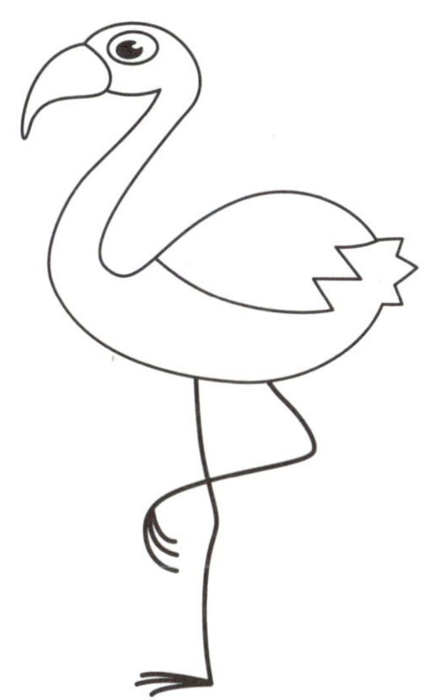

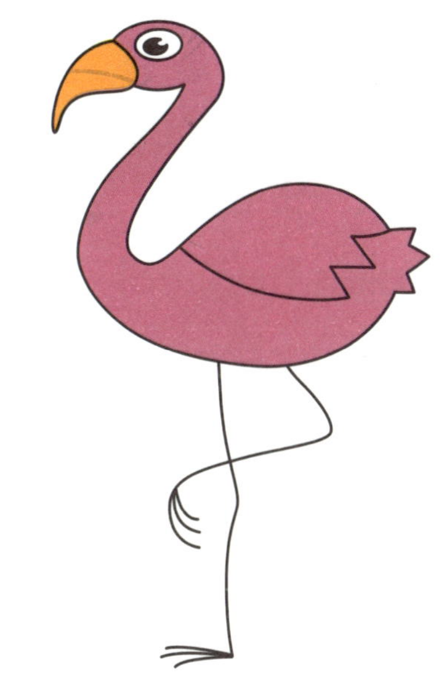

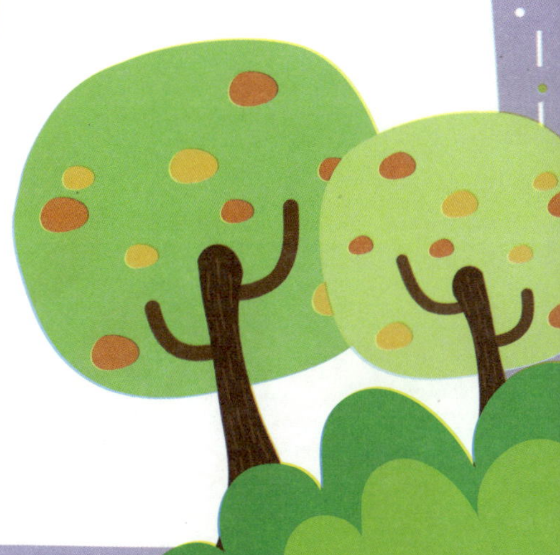

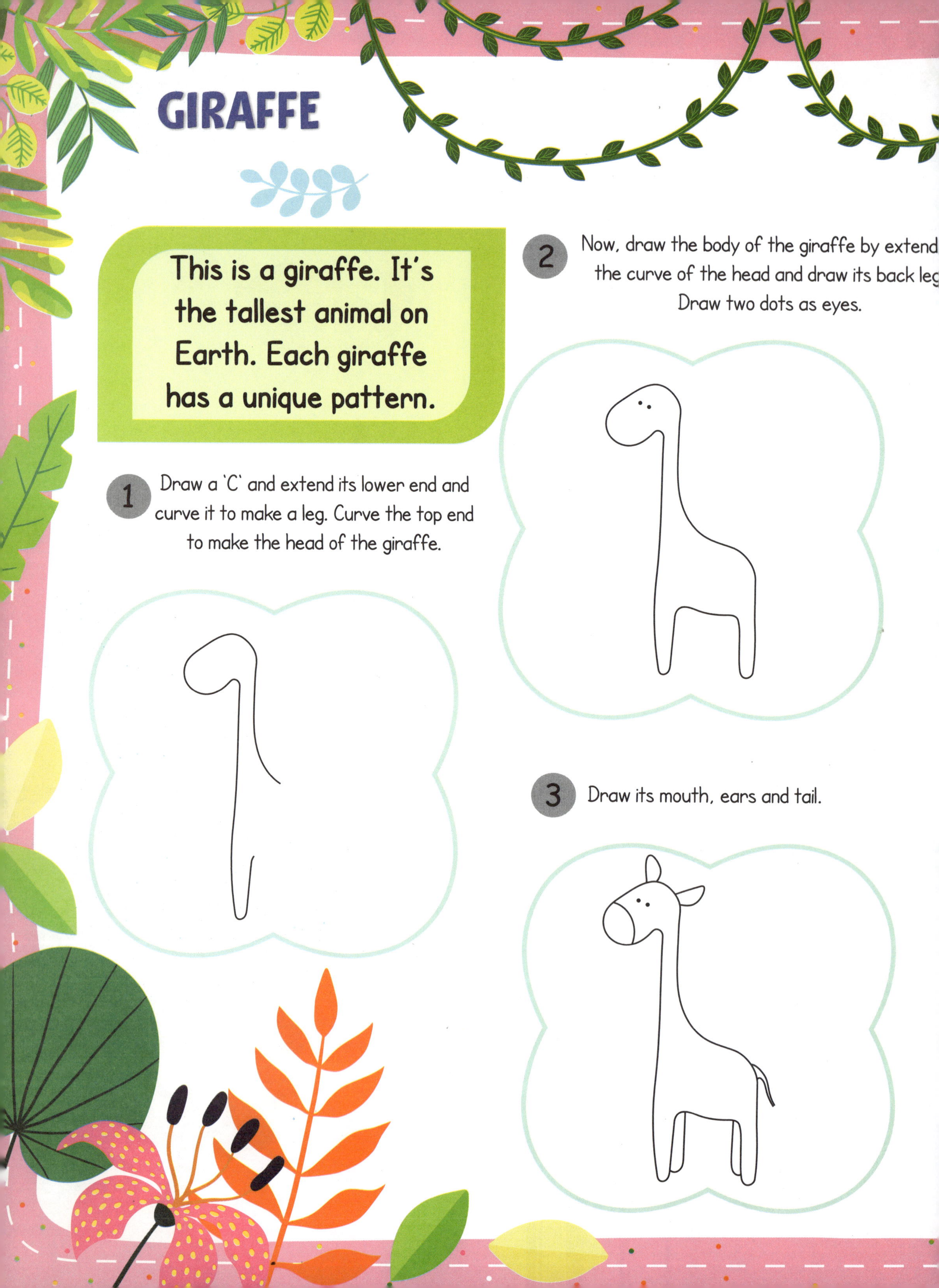

GIRAFFE

This is a giraffe. It's the tallest animal on Earth. Each giraffe has a unique pattern.

1 Draw a 'C' and extend its lower end and curve it to make a leg. Curve the top end to make the head of the giraffe.

2 Now, draw the body of the giraffe by extend the curve of the head and draw its back leg Draw two dots as eyes.

3 Draw its mouth, ears and tail.

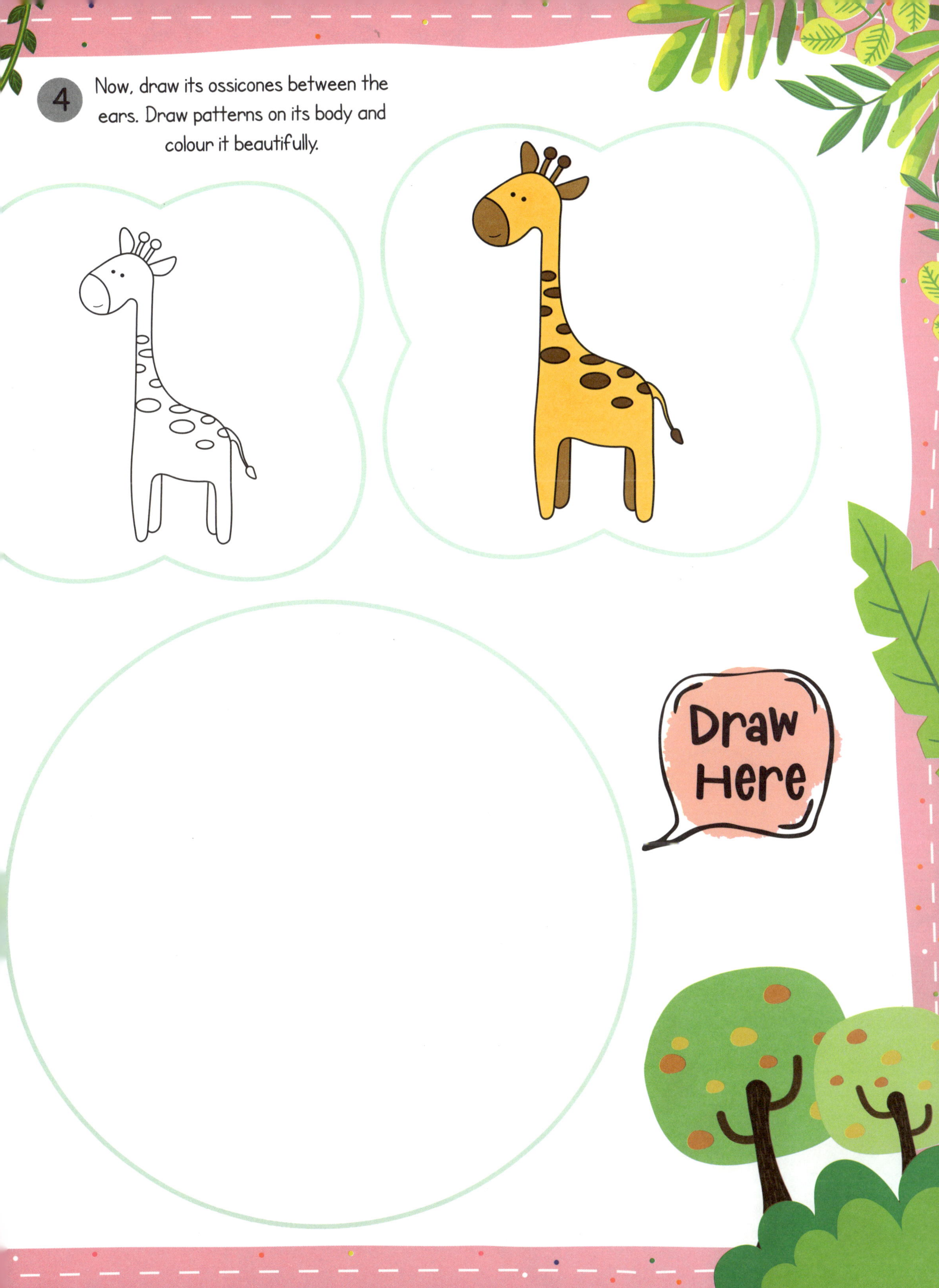
4
Now, draw its ossicones between the ears. Draw patterns on its body and colour it beautifully.
Draw Here

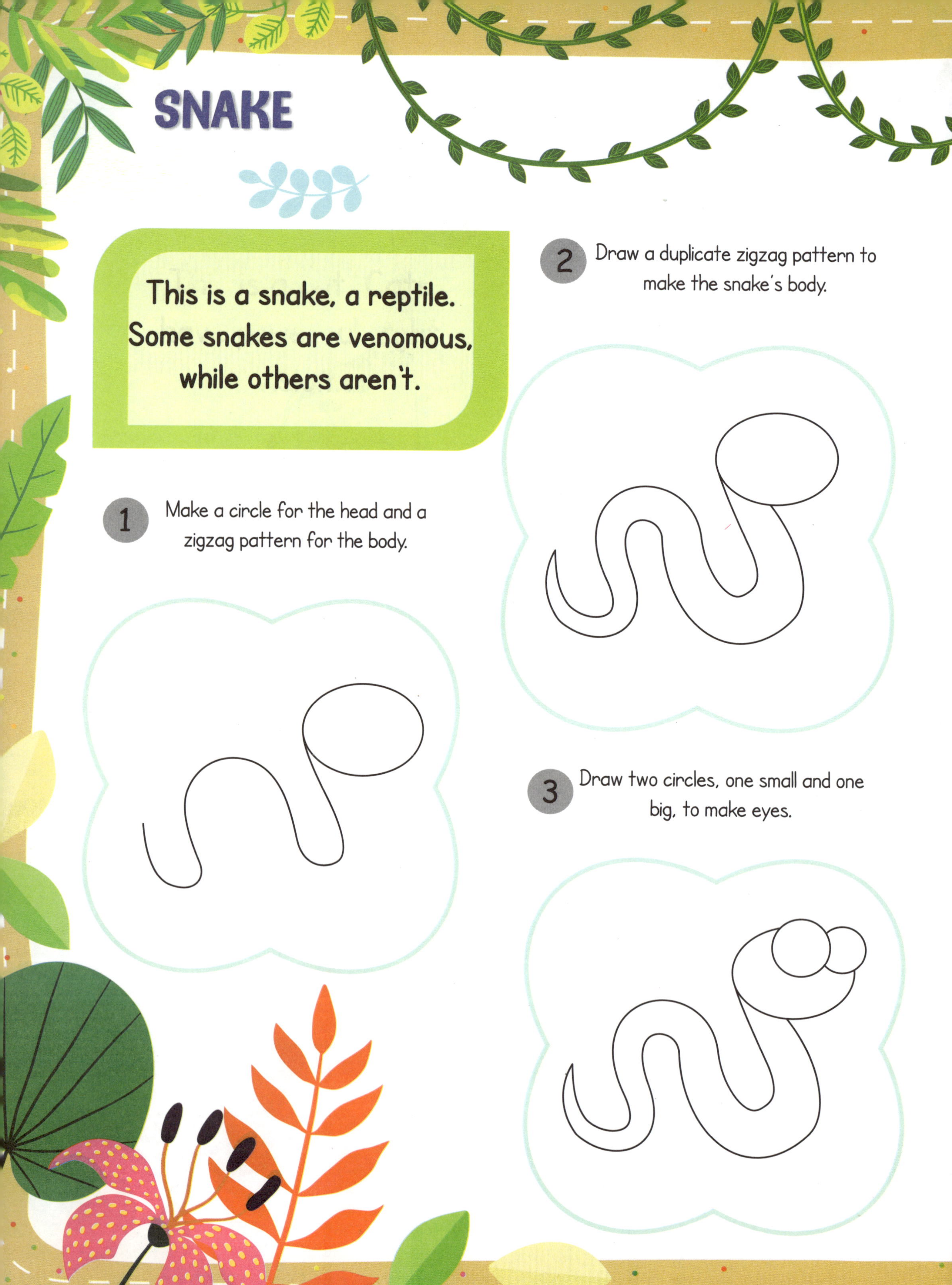

SNAKE

This is a snake, a reptile. Some snakes are venomous, while others aren't.

1 Make a circle for the head and a zigzag pattern for the body.

2 Draw a duplicate zigzag pattern to make the snake's body.

3 Draw two circles, one small and one big, to make eyes.

4 Make a mouth and a tongue. Draw eyeballs and more lines below the body.

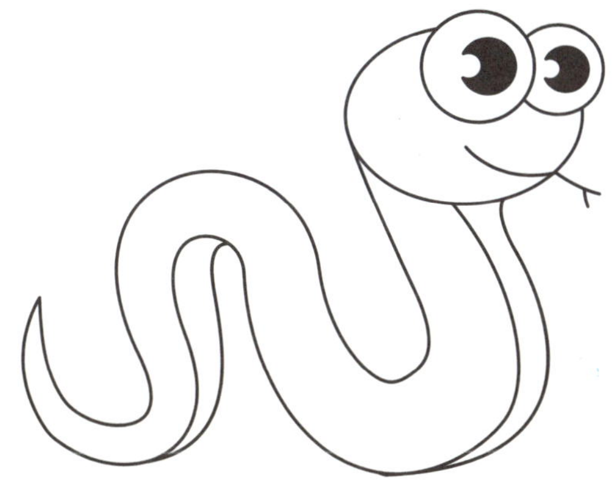

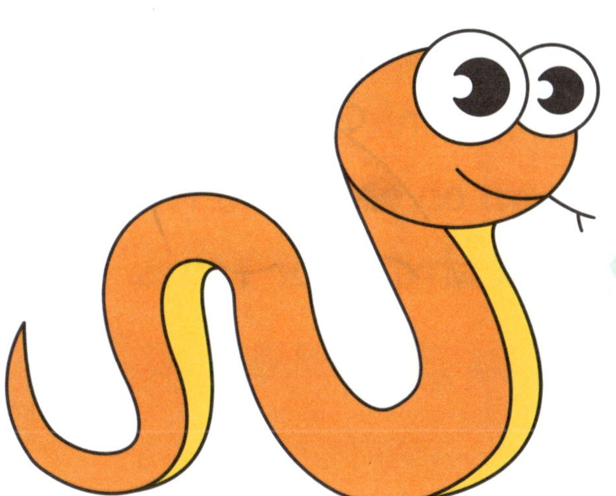

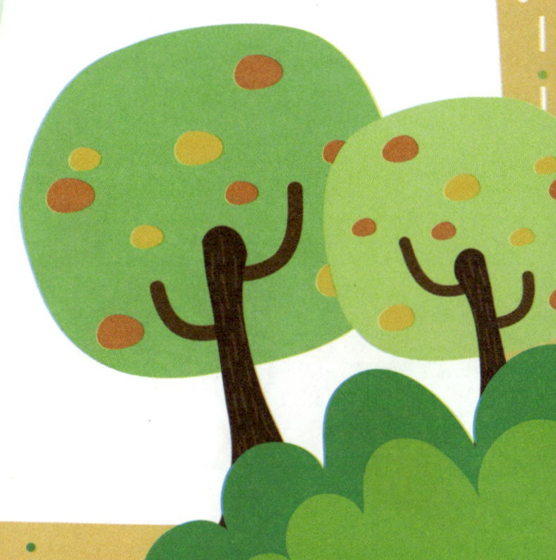

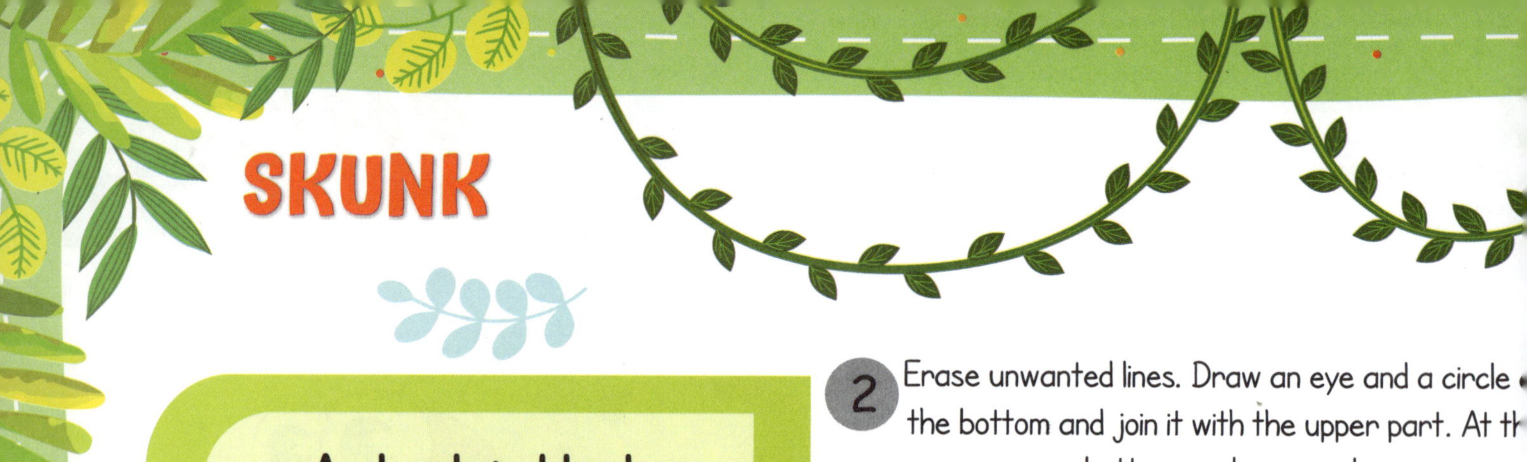

SKUNK

A skunk is black, brown or grey and has white stripes or spots.

1 Draw a circle for the face. Make a circle for the eye and eyeball. Draw the front face.

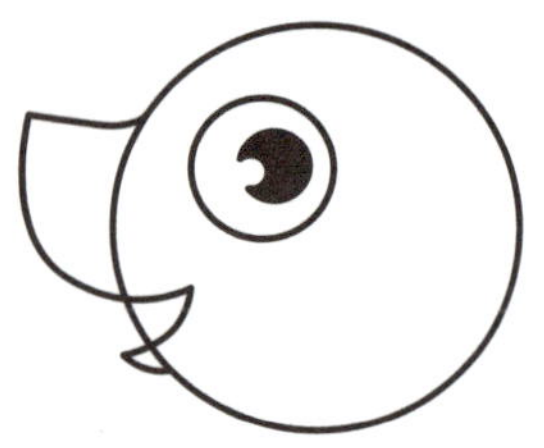

2 Erase unwanted lines. Draw an eye and a circle at the bottom and join it with the upper part. At the bottom, make an oval.

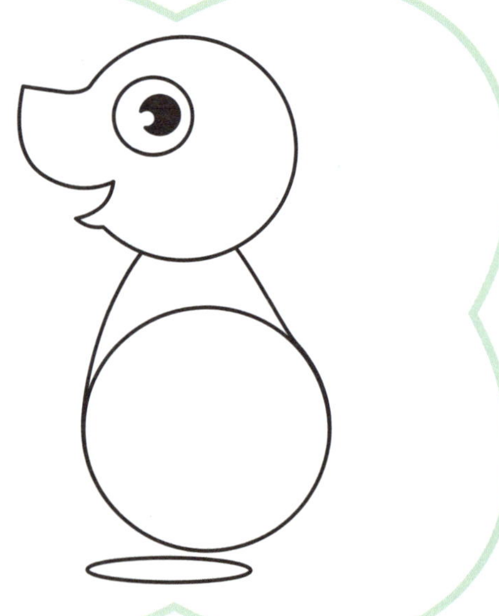

3 Draw an ear and the inside parts of the lower body. Make the foot.

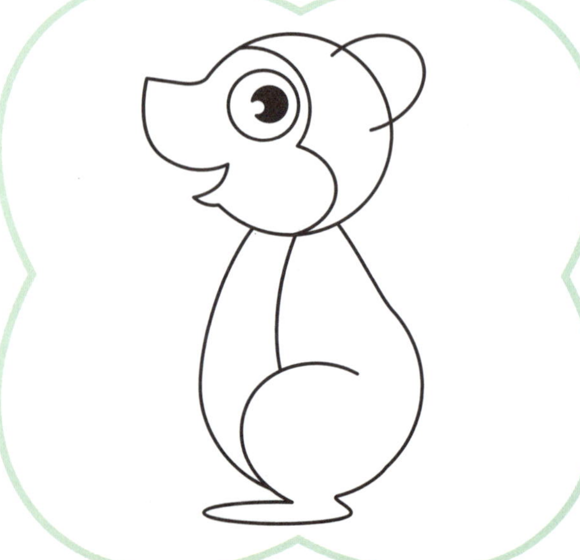

4 Draw a circle for the nose. Make hair, feet, a hand and a tail.

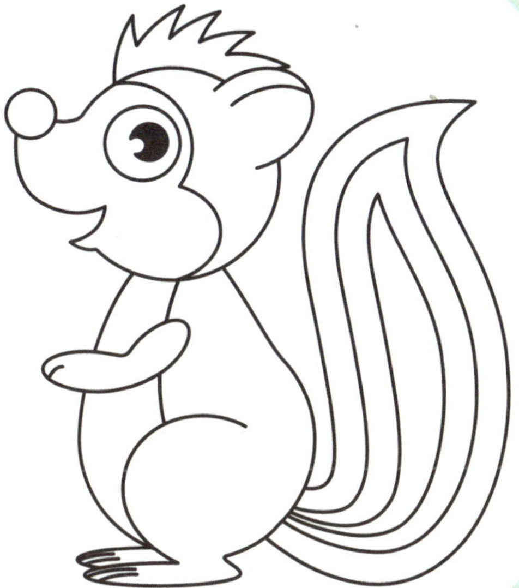

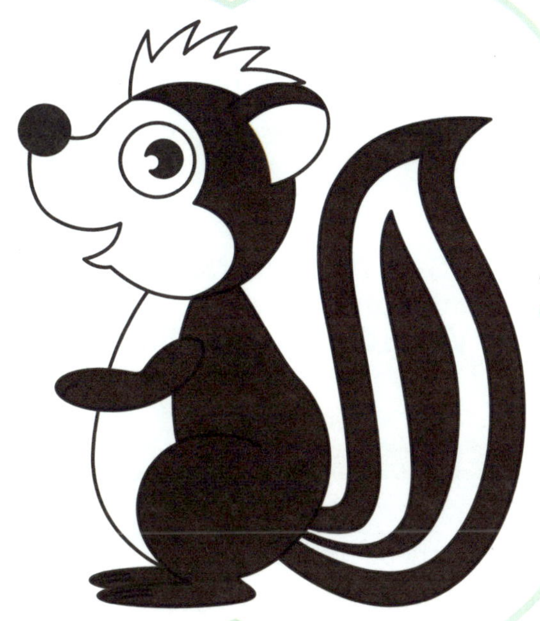

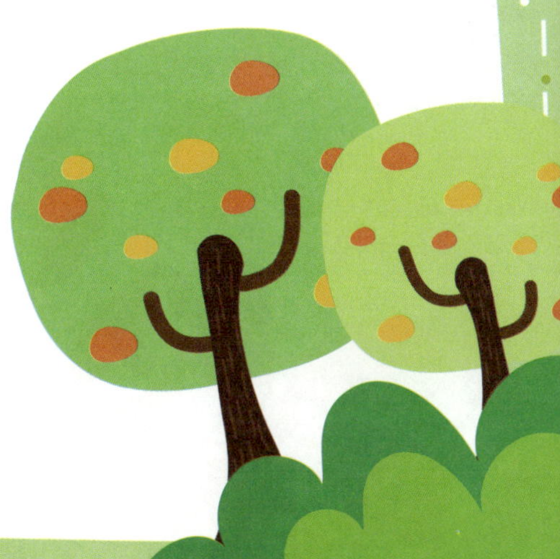

RACCOON

This is a raccoon. It is a very intelligent animal.

1 Draw a shape somewhat similar to an oval and below that, make a shape for the body.

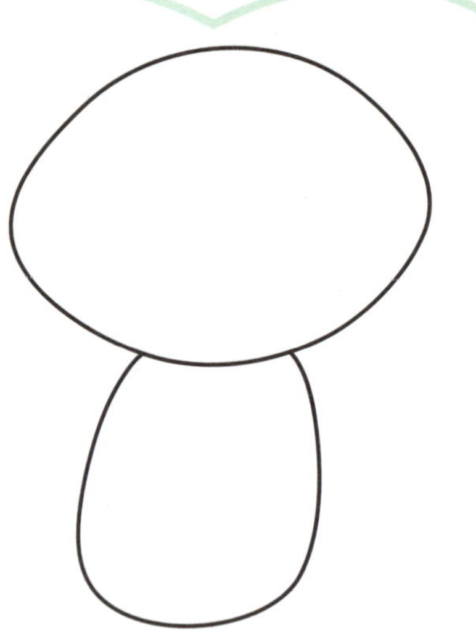

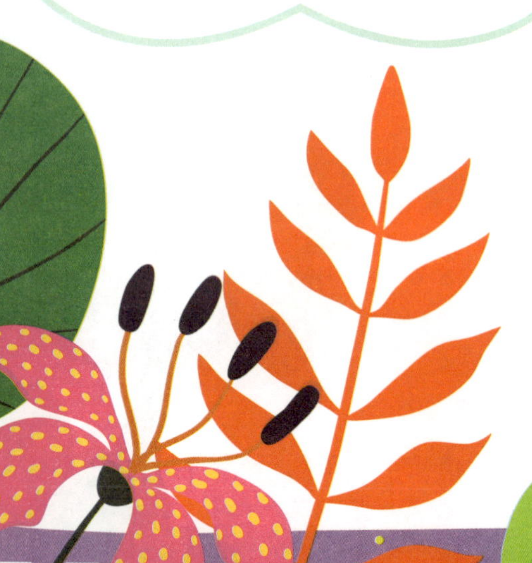

2 Draw ears, eyes, eyeballs and the inner part of the raccoon.

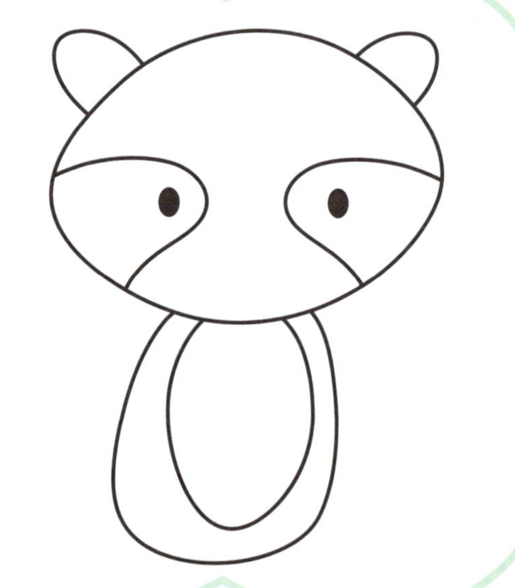

3 Draw the nose and hands on the inside part of the body.

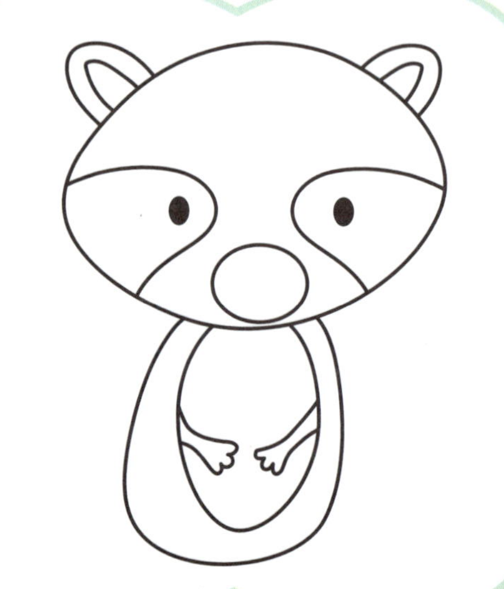

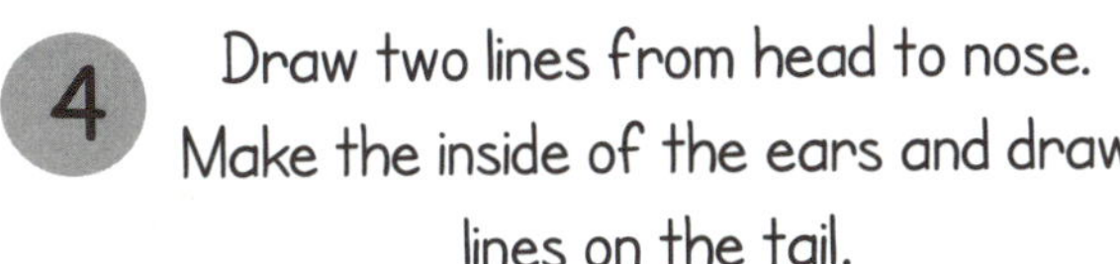

Draw two lines from head to nose. Make the inside of the ears and draw lines on the tail.

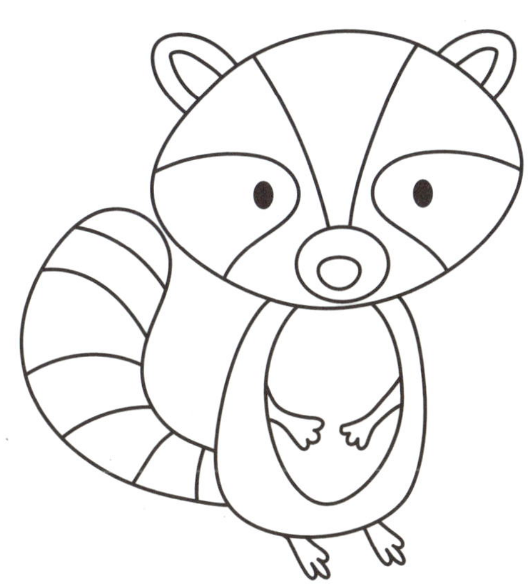

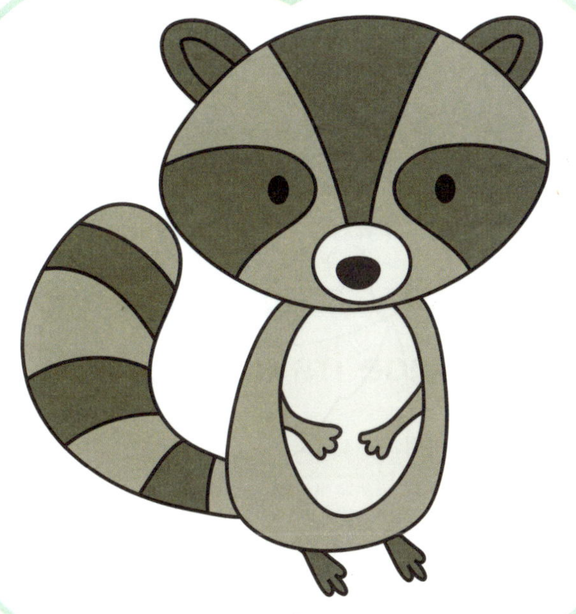

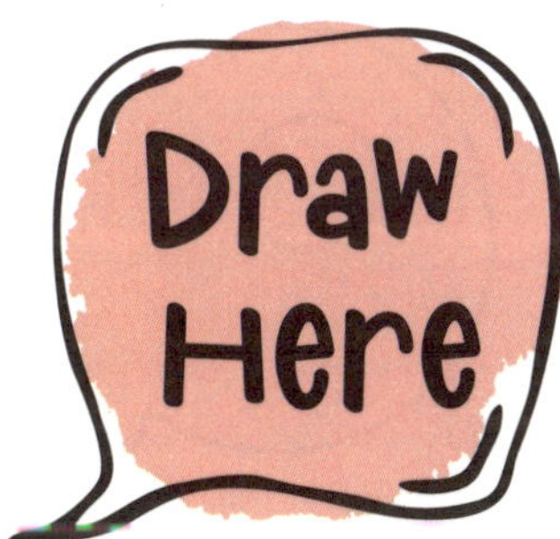

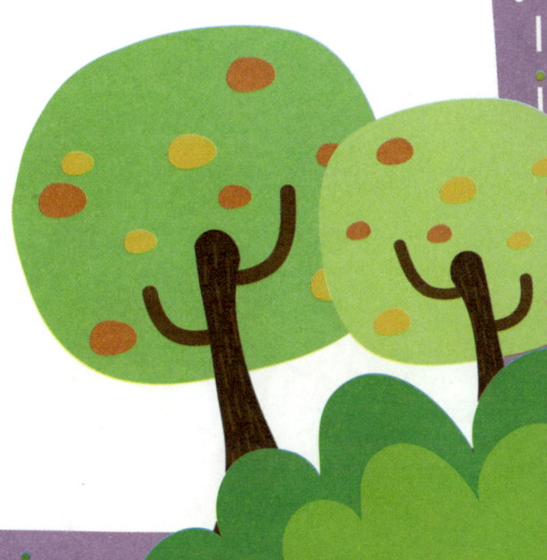

CHAMELEON

This is a chameleon. It has a sticky tongue and can change its colour.

1 Draw a shape like number 8 with the upper part a little bigger and make a small circle inside it.

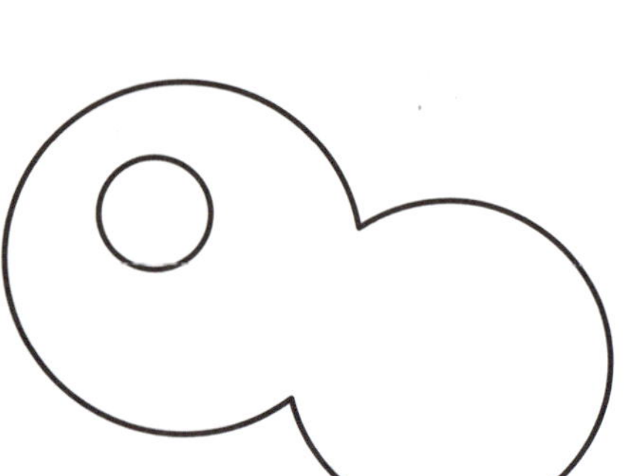

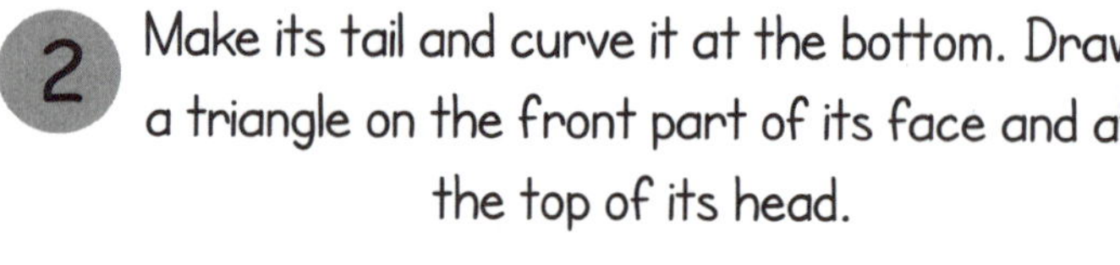

2 Make its tail and curve it at the bottom. Draw a triangle on the front part of its face and at the top of its head.

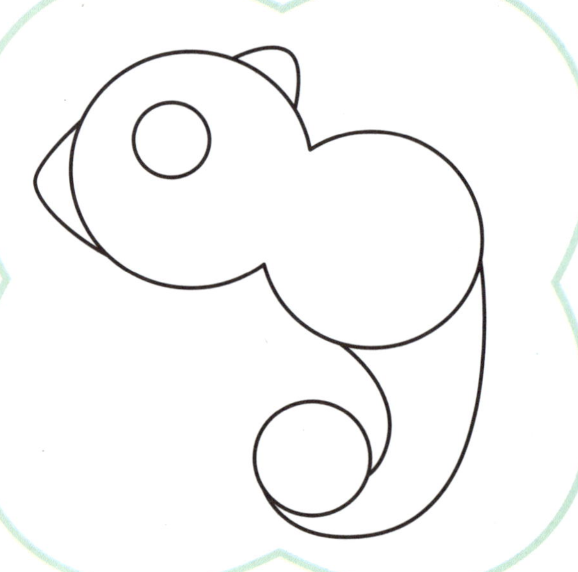

3 Make a tail at the bottom of the circle and remove unwanted lines.

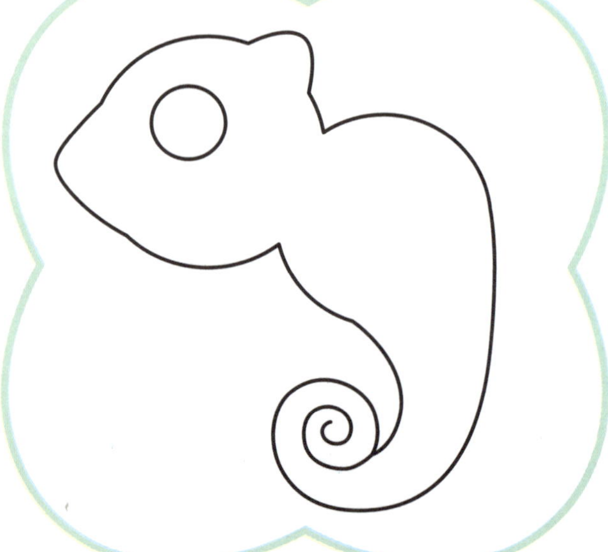

4 Draw the mouth, arms and hands.
Draw a curved line for making a log.

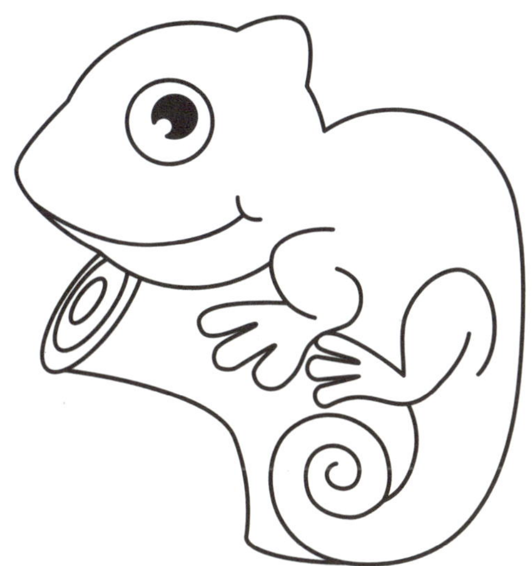

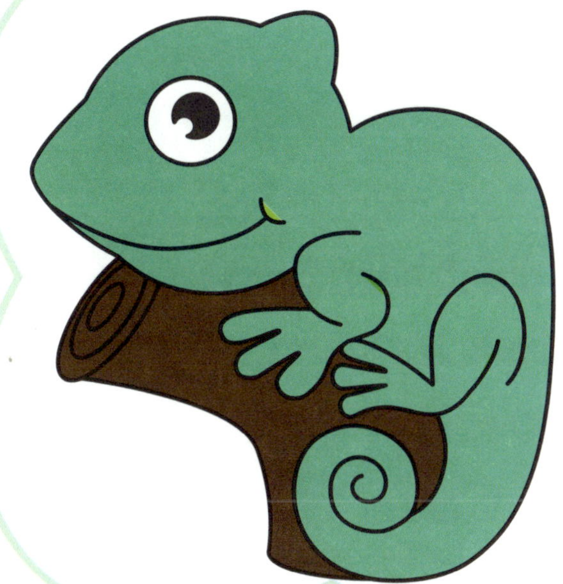

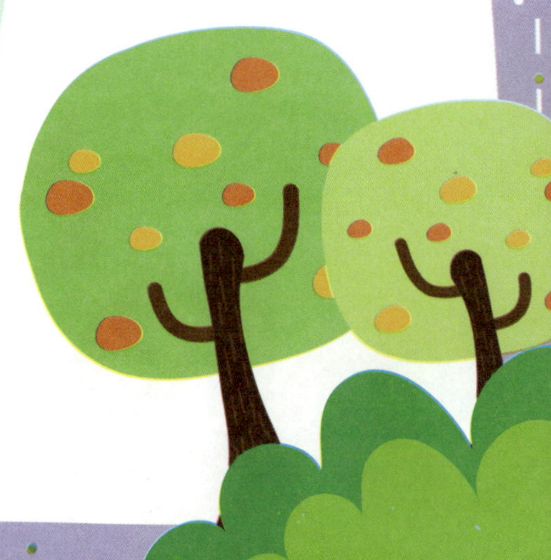

RHINOCEROS

This is a rhinoceros. Its giant horn grows from its snout.

1 Make a circle for the face of the rhino. Draw its horn in the circle.

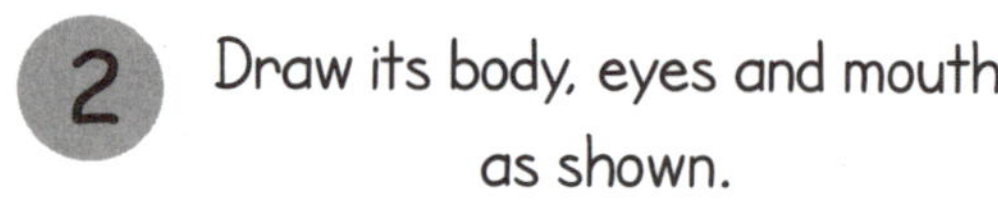

2 Draw its body, eyes and mouth as shown.

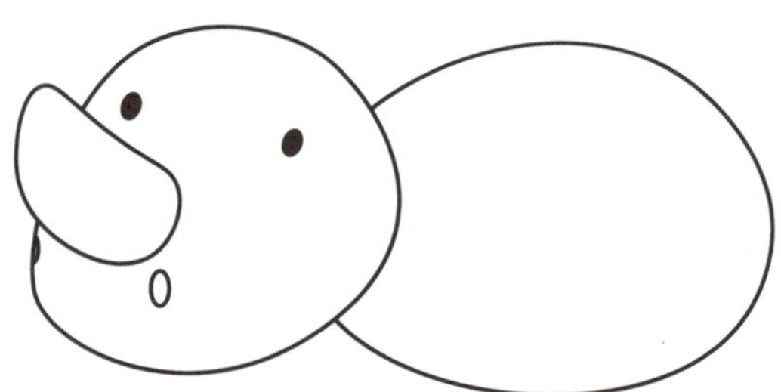

3 Now, draw its legs and ears.

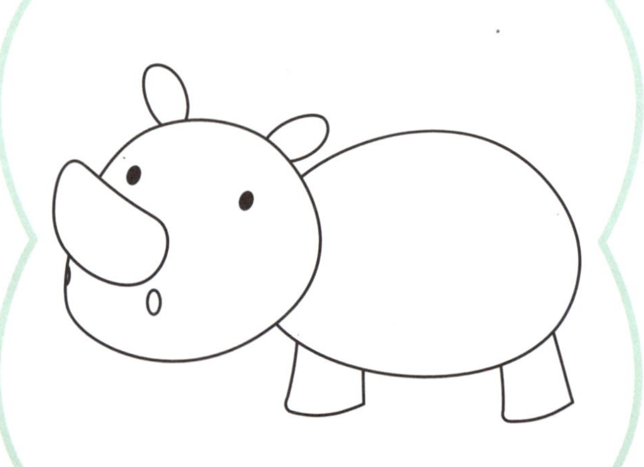

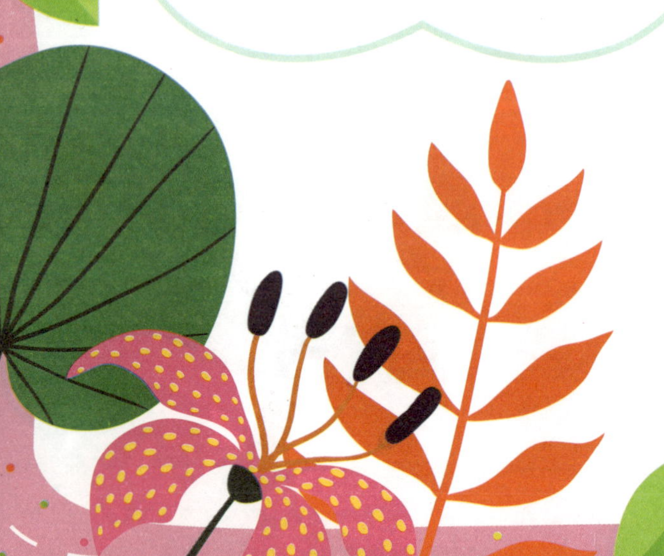

4 Draw the details on its legs and ears.
Complete the rhino by drawing its tail.

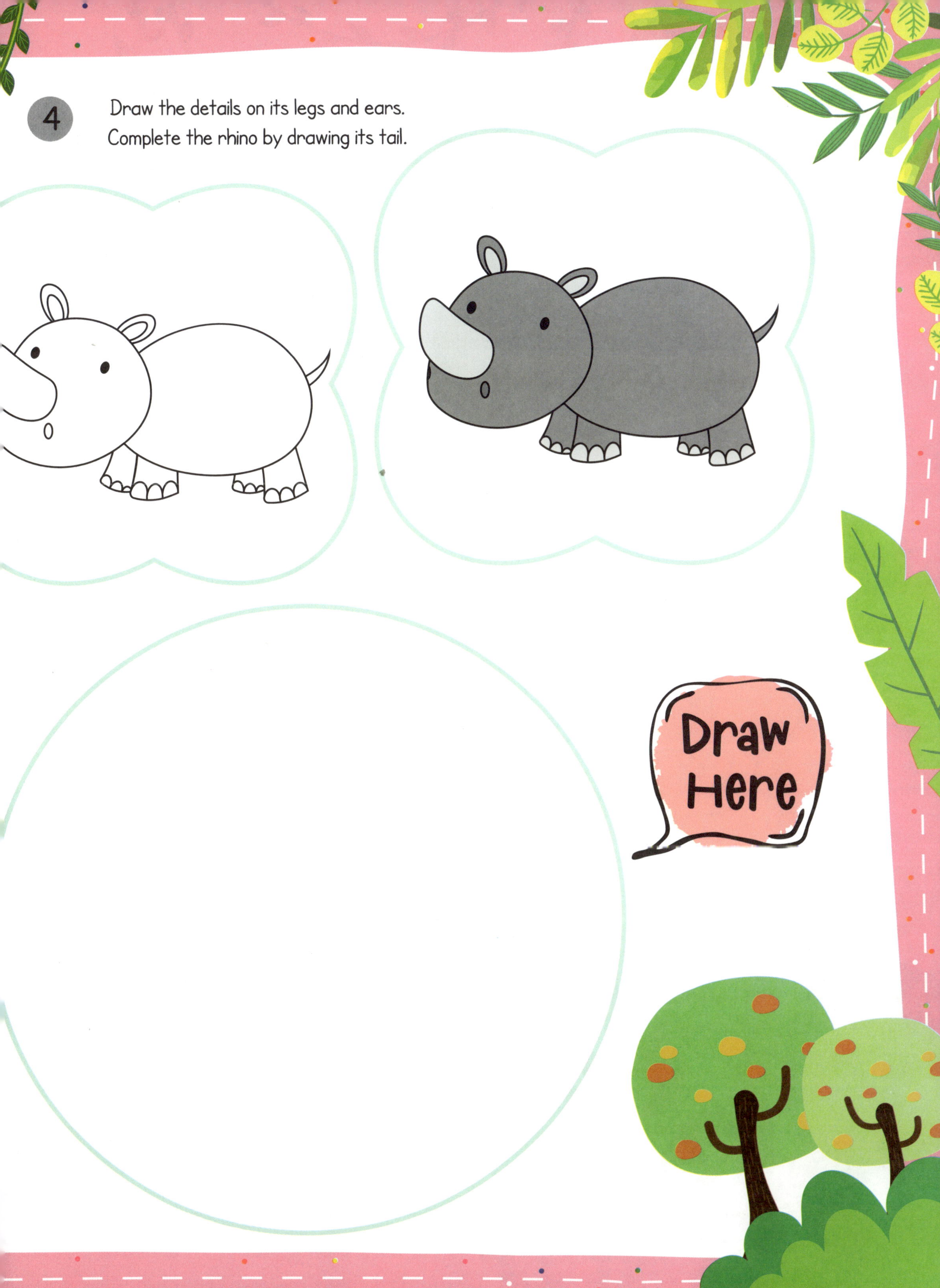

VULTURE

This is a vulture. They are scavengers and are found all over the world.

1 Draw a circle and then a neck. Make a triangle with curved ends for the body.

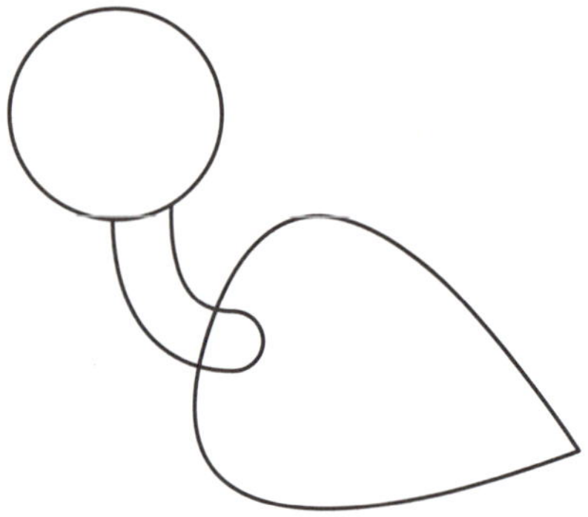

2 Inside the circle draw eyes and a beak.

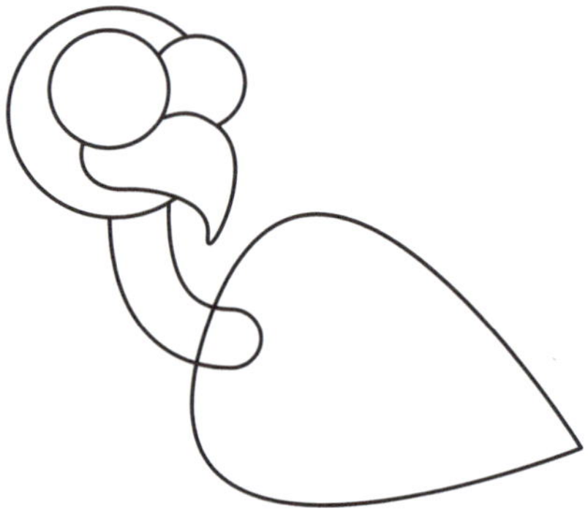

3 Draw three lines for hair and one curved line inside the beak. Draw legs, feet and a tail.

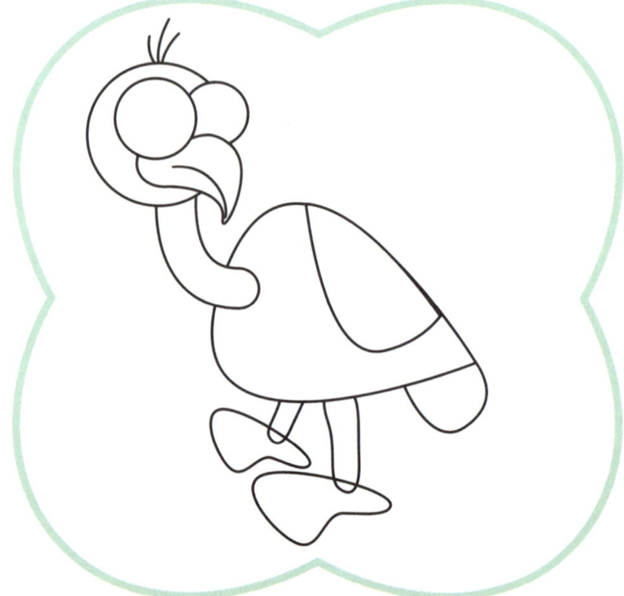

4 Draw eyeballs. Make curves for feathers, feet and a tail.

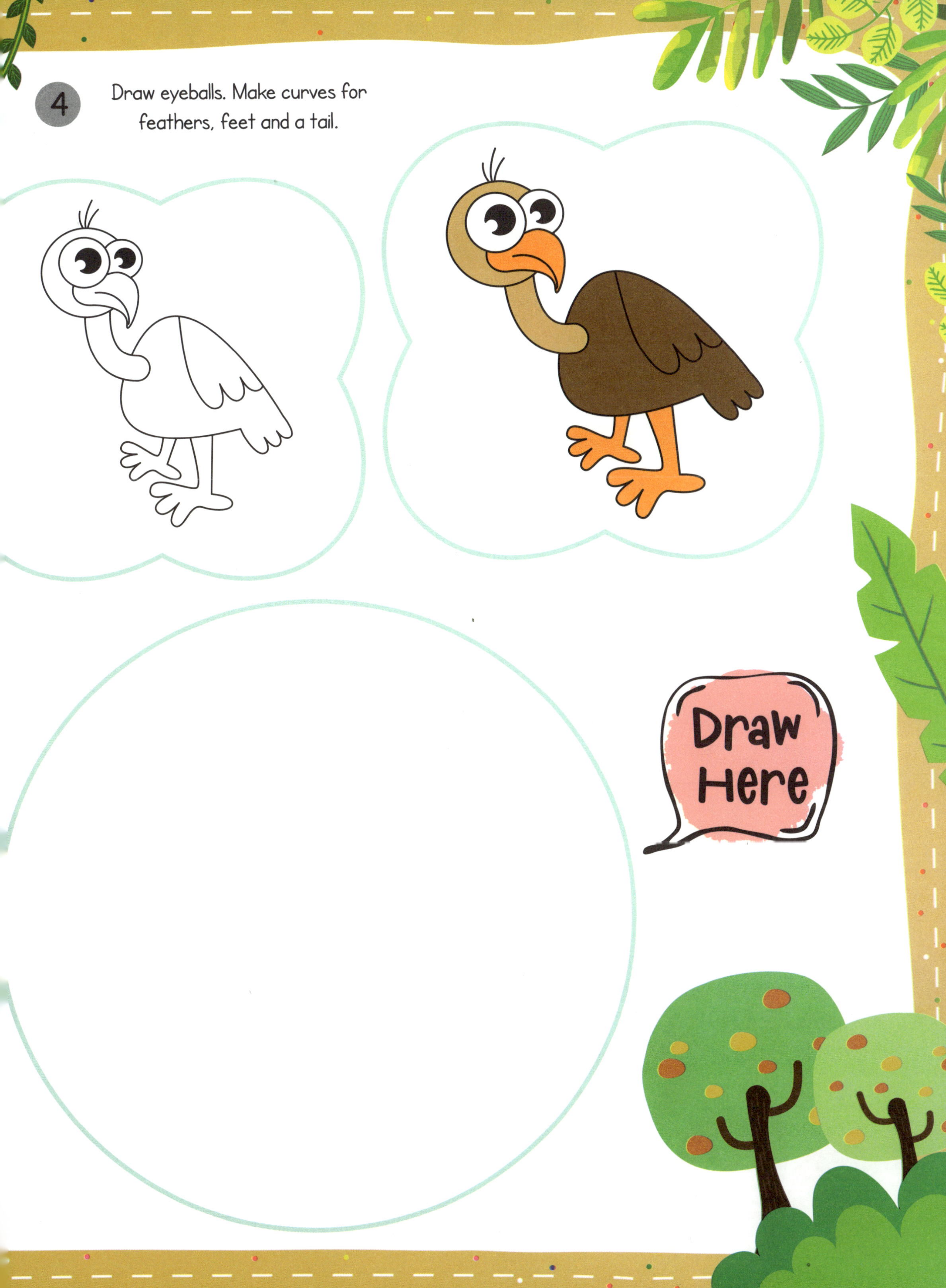

SQUIRREL

This is a squirrel. It likes to eat nuts. Acorns are its favourite food.

1 Draw a semi-circle to make the face of a squirrel. Draw its mouth and nose in the middle.

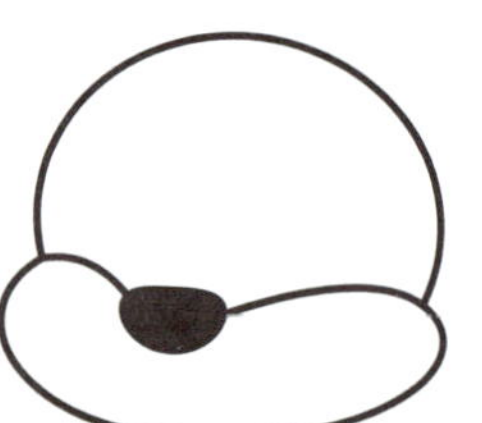

2 Draw its body from its neck in a sitting position.

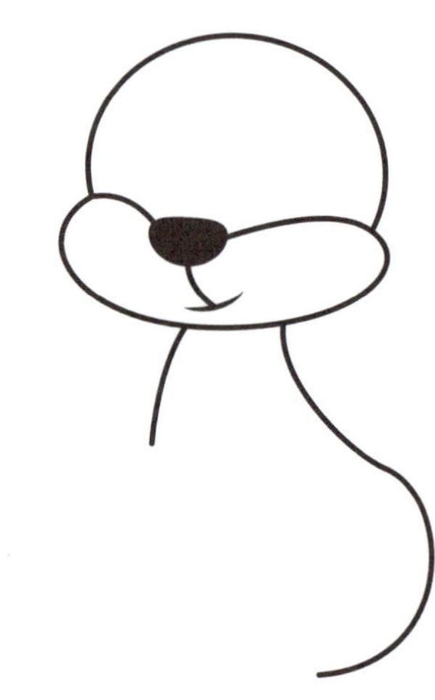

3 Draw its eyes, ears, mouth and body.

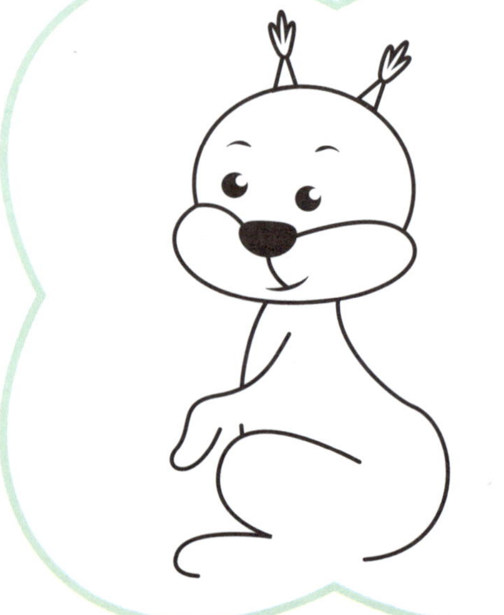

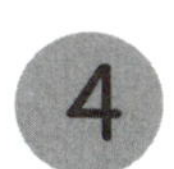

4 After completing the body, draw its tail and colour it.

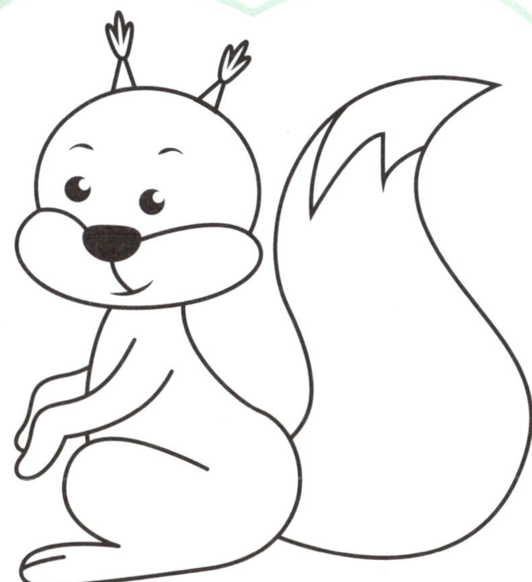

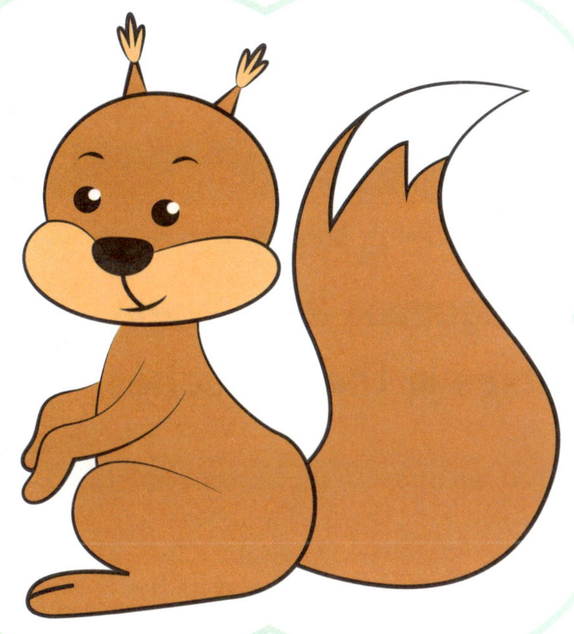

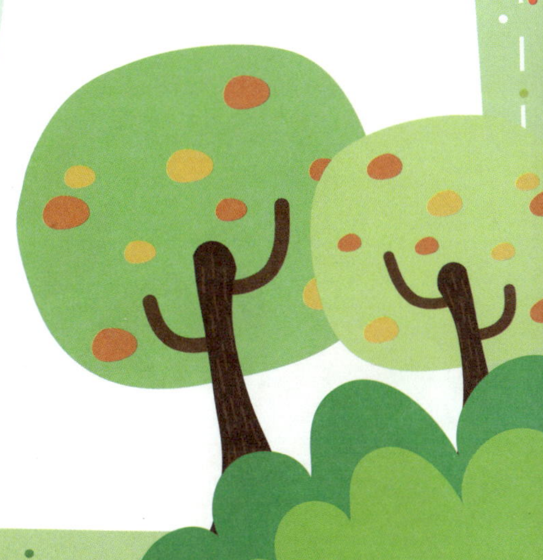

KANGAROO

This is a kangaroo. Kangaroos keep their babies in their pouches.

1 Make one circle and one oval at the top of it. Join them with two curved lines.

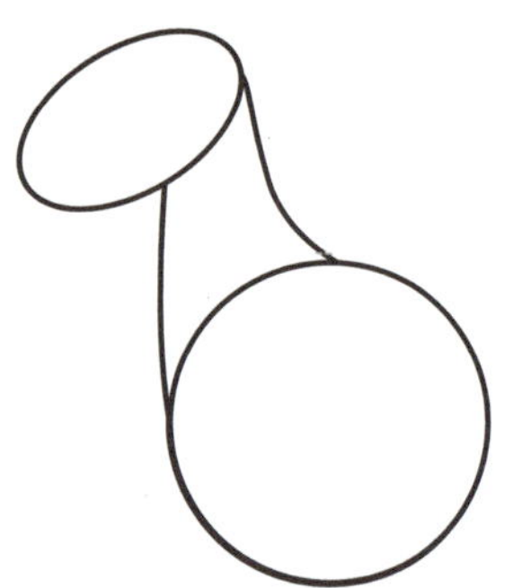

2 Draw an eye, an eyeball and a mouth. Draw two lines for the legs and an oval at the bottom.

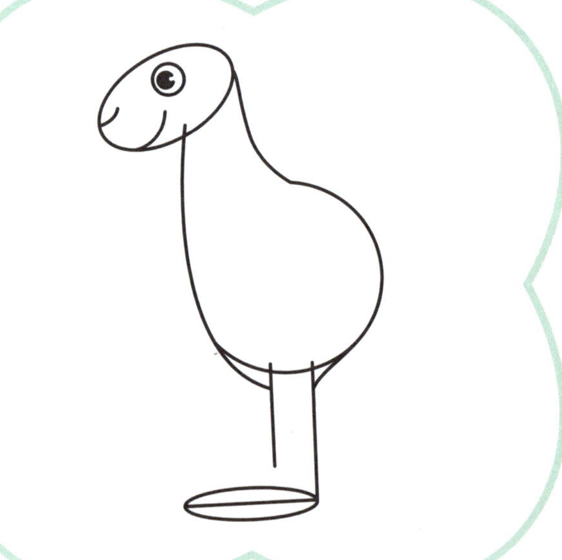

3 Make the kangaroo's arm and foot. Erase unwanted lines.

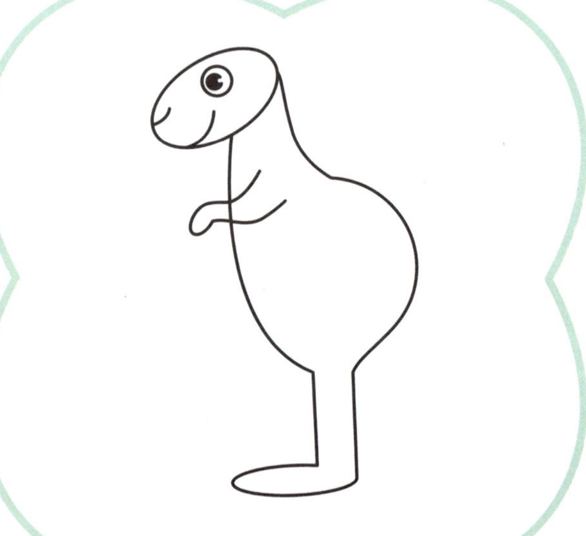

4 Draw ears, a second hand and a tail. Draw lines to make claws on the feet and hands.

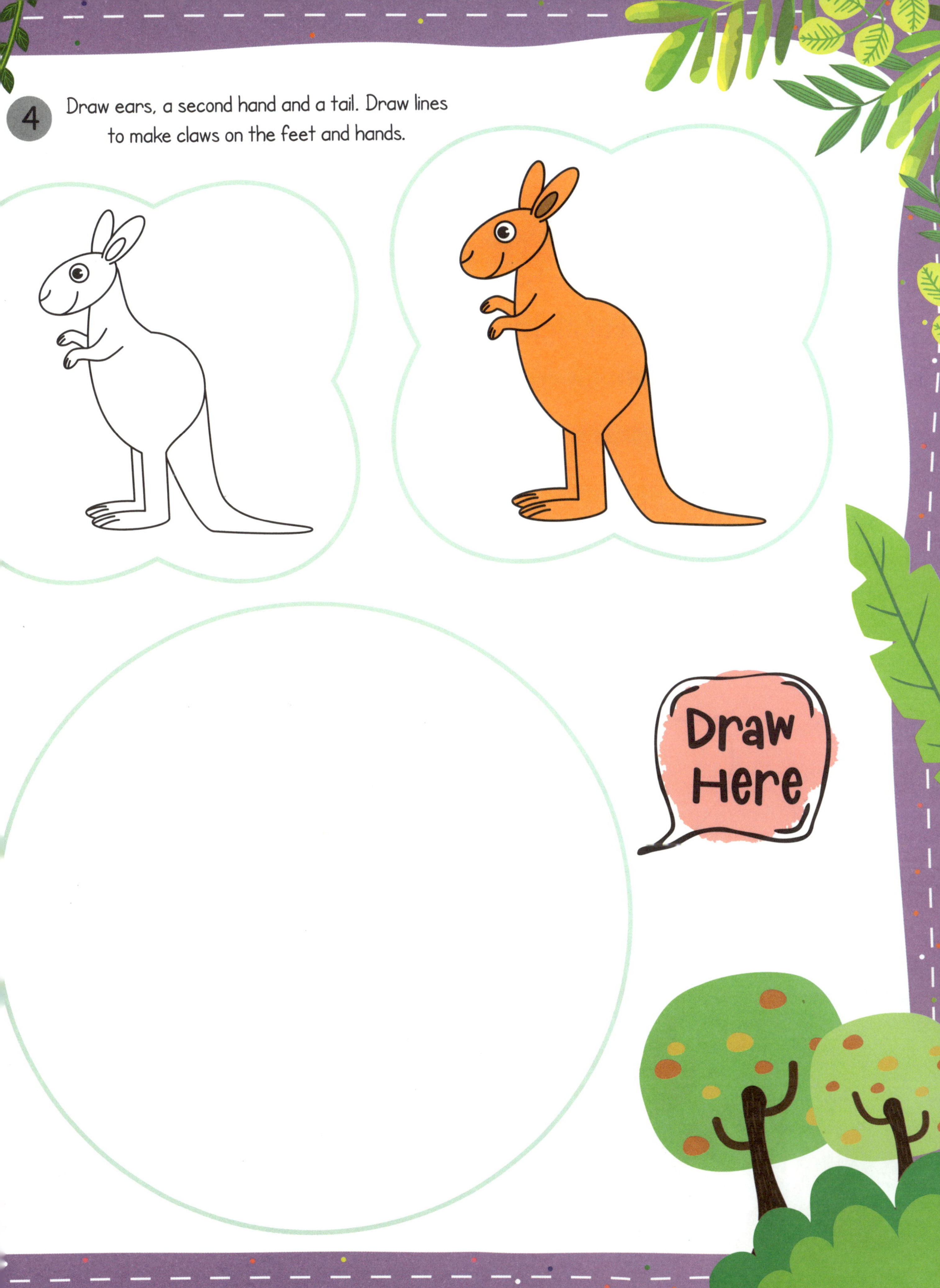

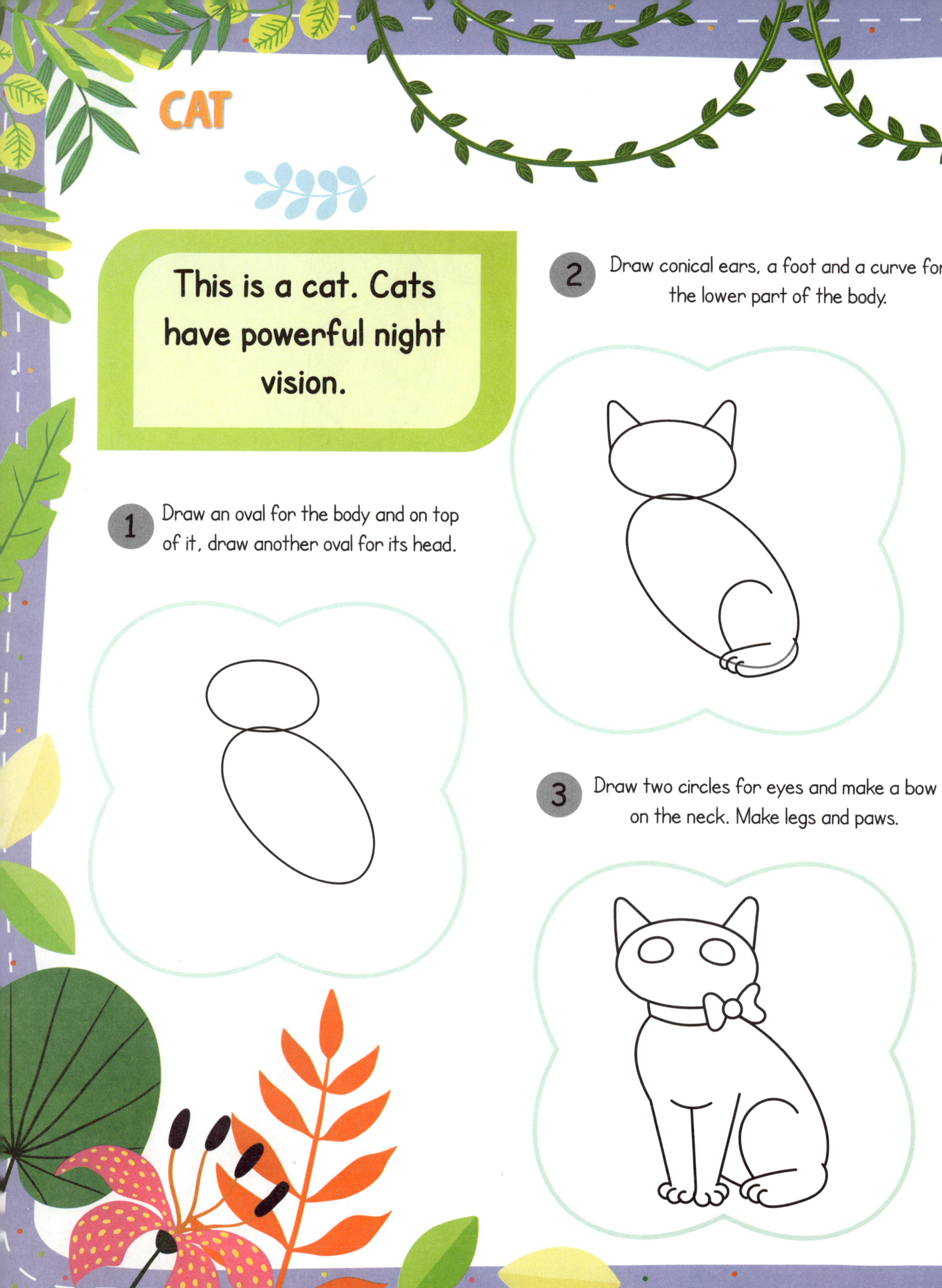

CAT

This is a cat. Cats have powerful night vision.

1. Draw an oval for the body and on top of it, draw another oval for its head.

2. Draw conical ears, a foot and a curve for the lower part of the body.

3. Draw two circles for eyes and make a bow on the neck. Make legs and paws.

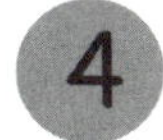

4 Draw eyeballs and a tail.

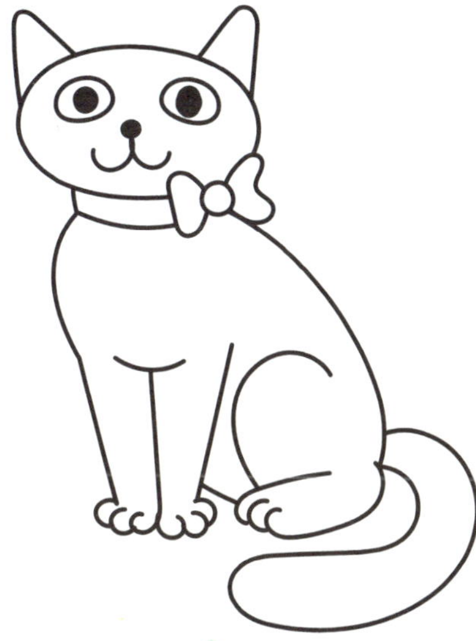

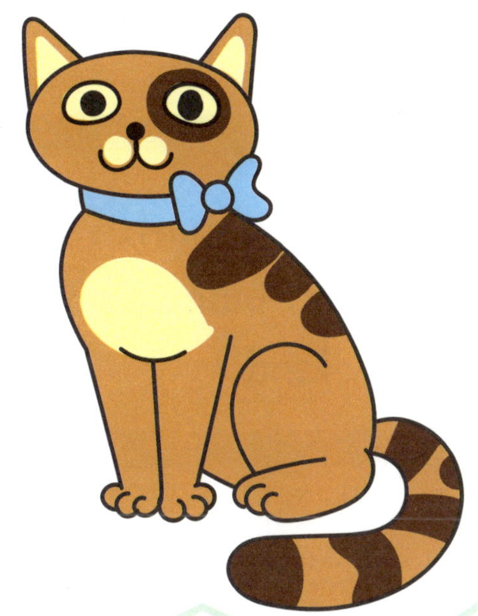

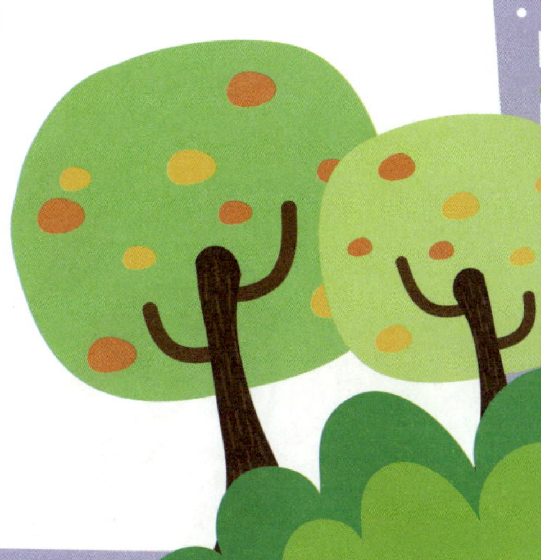

ELEPHANT

This is an elephant. It's the largest mammal on land.

1 Draw a slight oval shape for the face. Make eyes and eyeballs. Make an ear on the head.

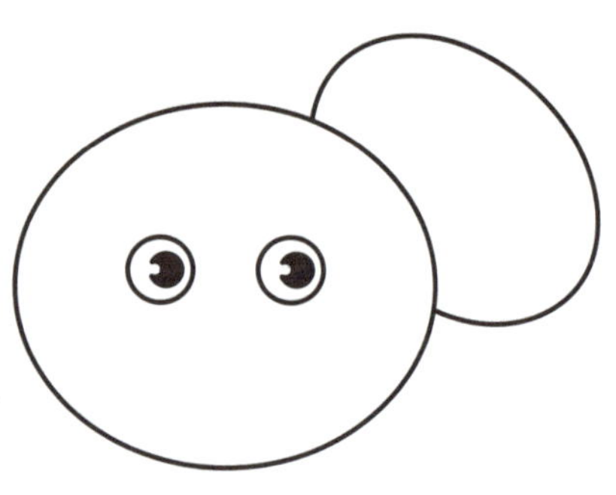

2 Draw a half-oval for the second ear. Draw two lines from the center of the face to make the elephant's trunk.

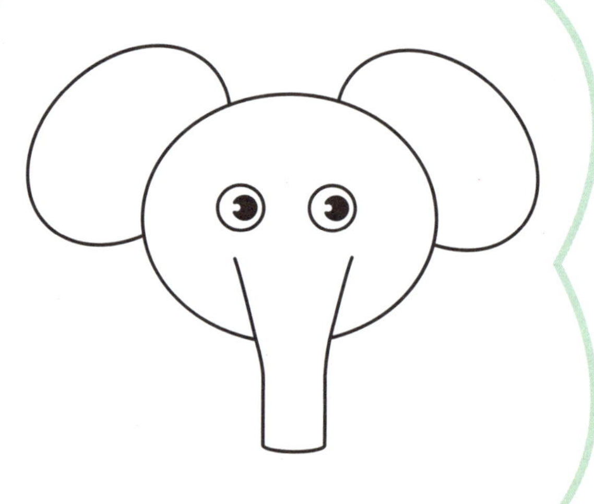

3 Below the left ear, draw the shape of the body.

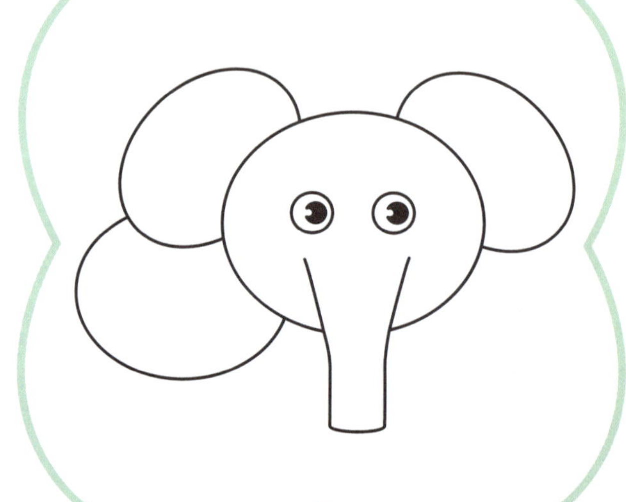

4 Draw feet and a tail.

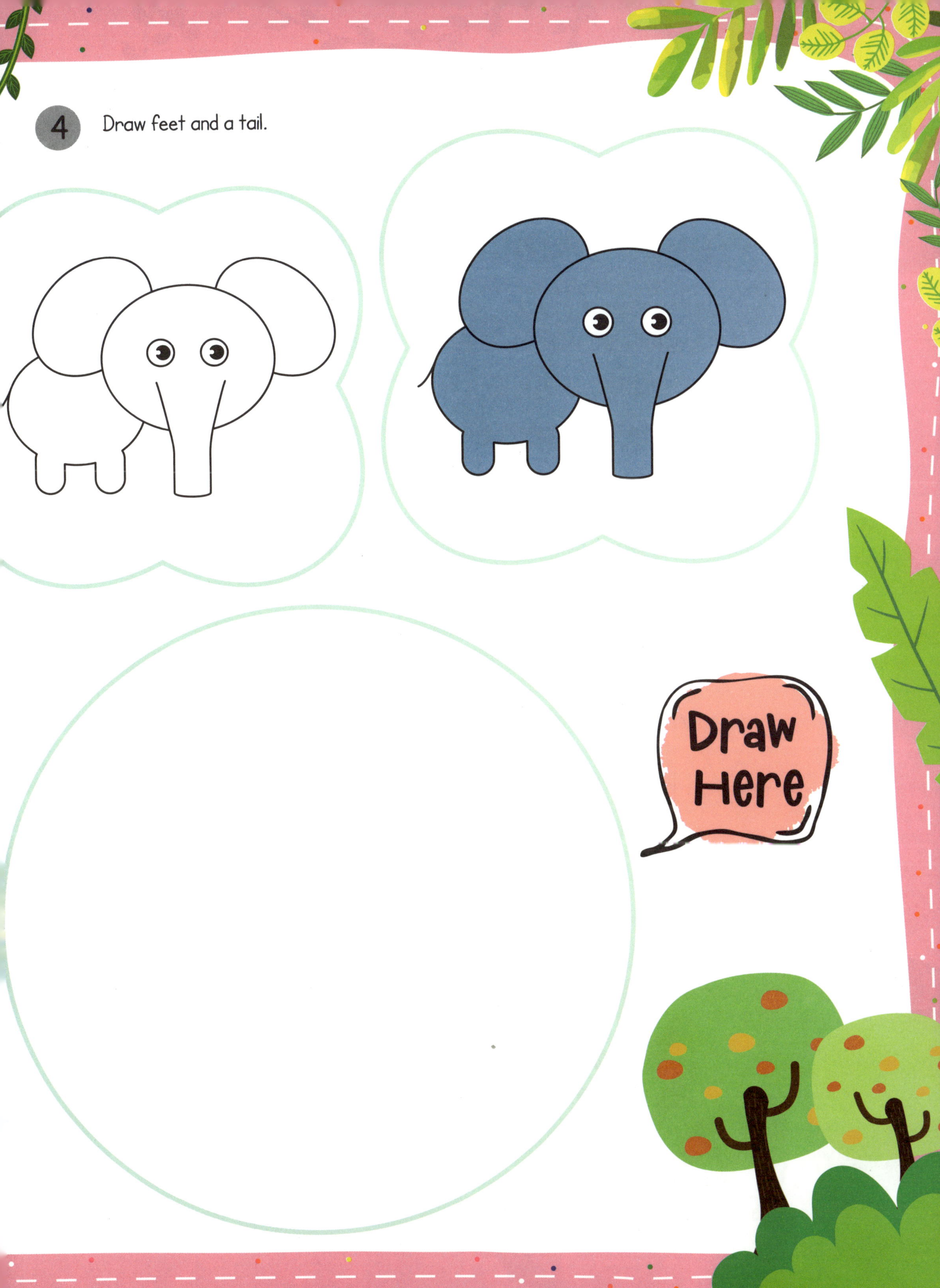

FOX

This is a fox. It has pointed ears. It hunts at night.

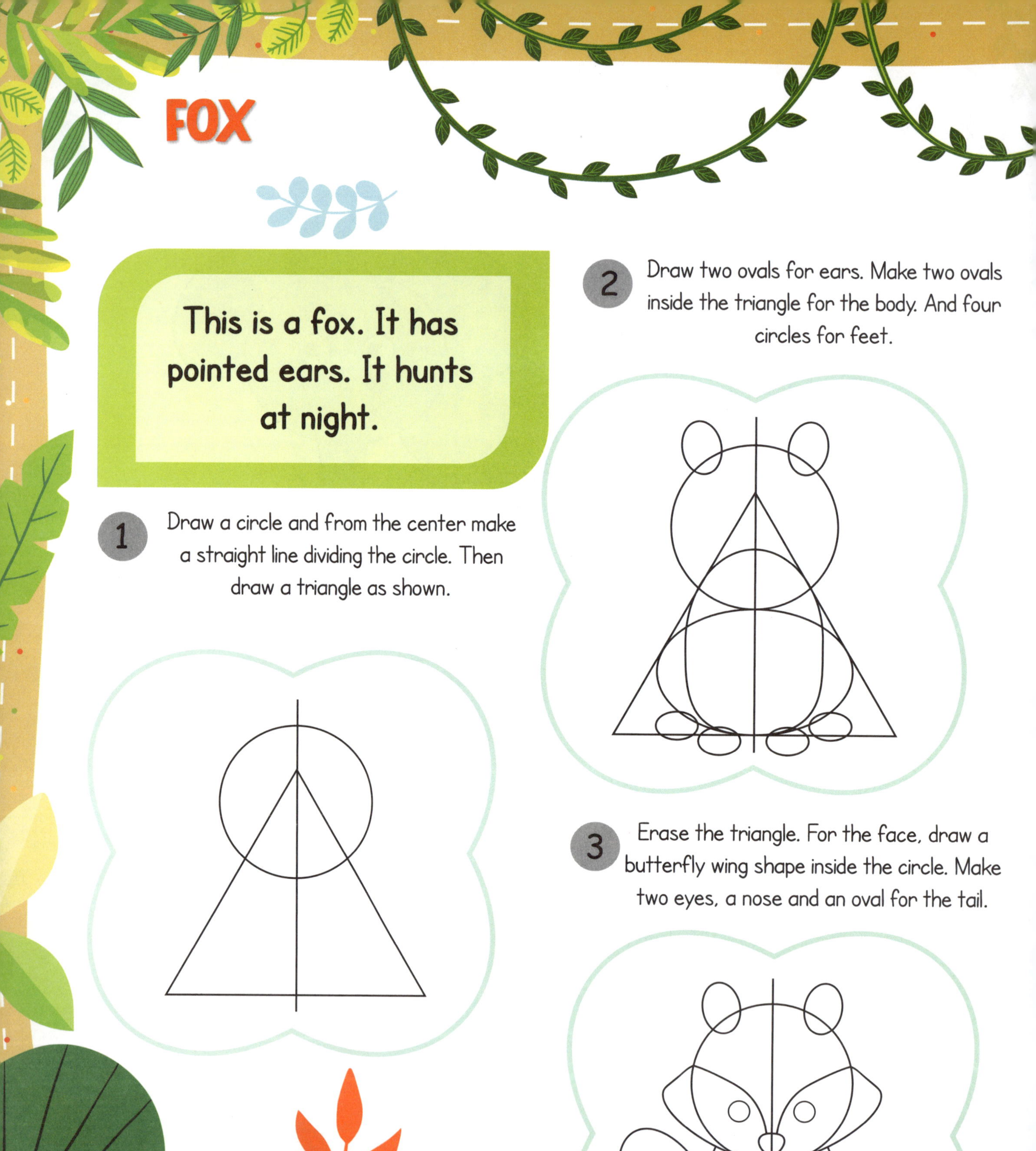

1 Draw a circle and from the center make a straight line dividing the circle. Then draw a triangle as shown.

2 Draw two ovals for ears. Make two ovals inside the triangle for the body. And four circles for feet.

3 Erase the triangle. For the face, draw a butterfly wing shape inside the circle. Make two eyes, a nose and an oval for the tail.

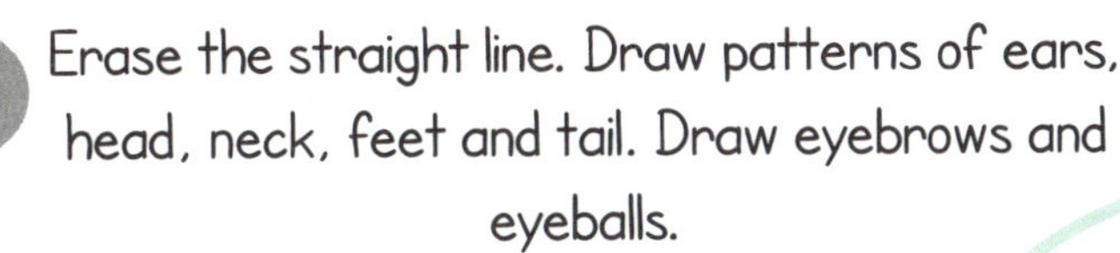

4 Erase the straight line. Draw patterns of ears, head, neck, feet and tail. Draw eyebrows and eyeballs.

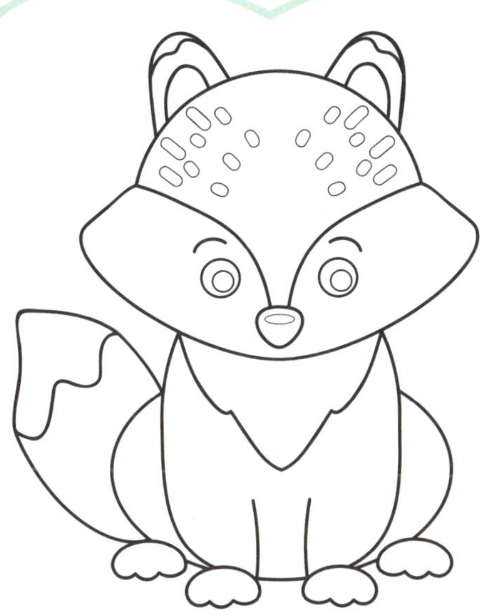

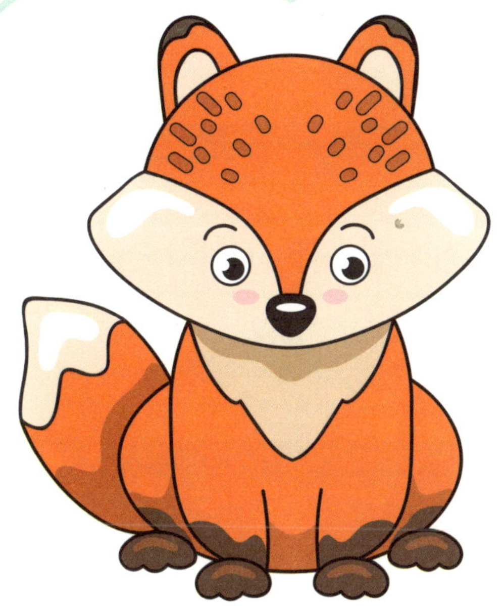

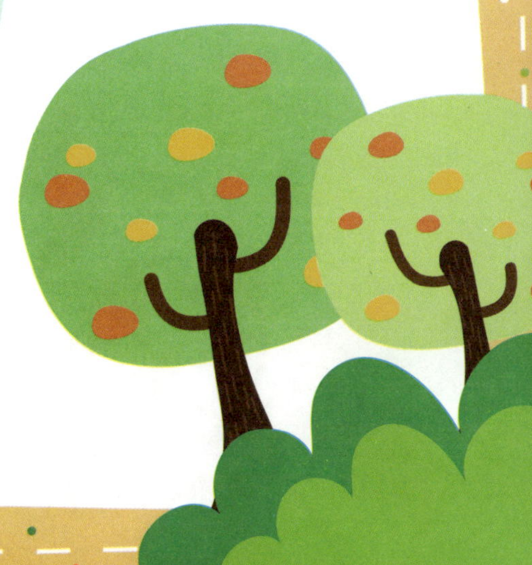

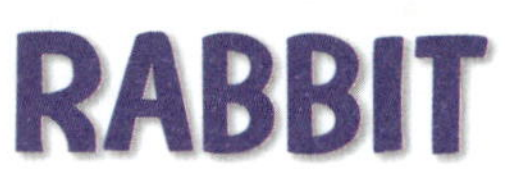

RABBIT

This is a rabbit. It lives in a burrow.

1 Draw an oval shape for the head of the rabbit.

2 Draw its body, eyes and ears.

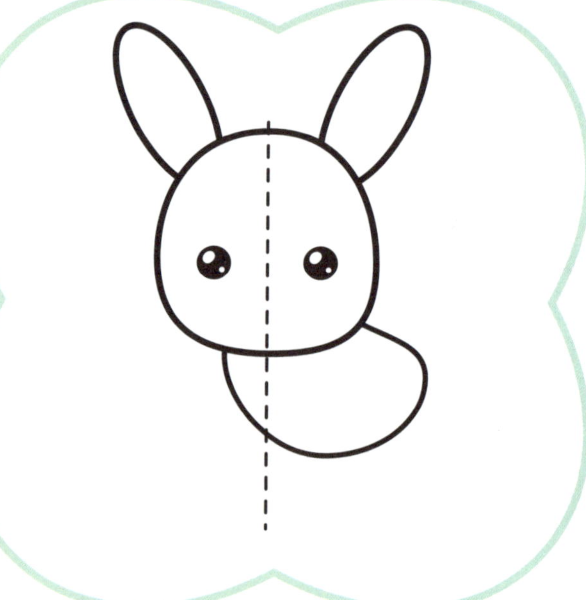

3 Draw its legs, nose and mouth. Draw details on its ears.

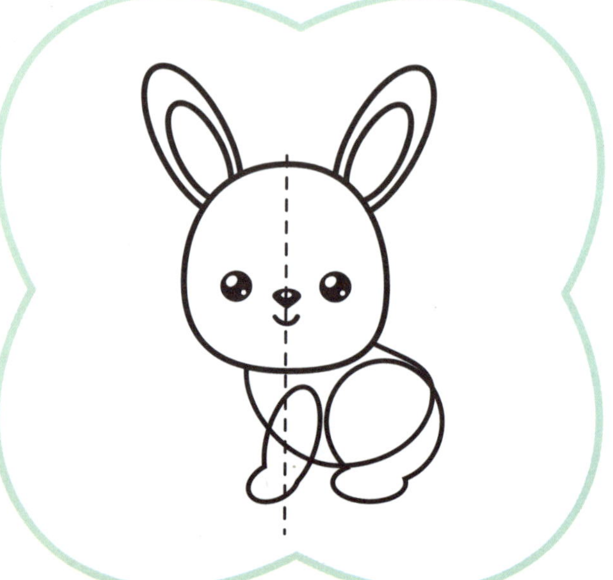

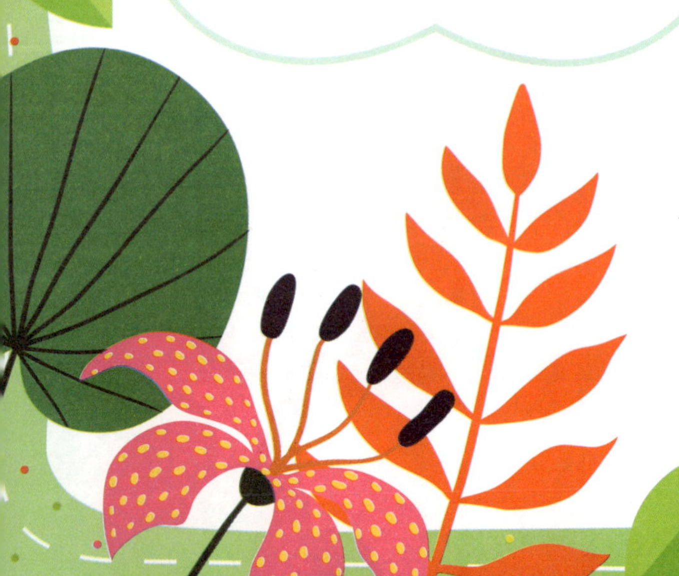

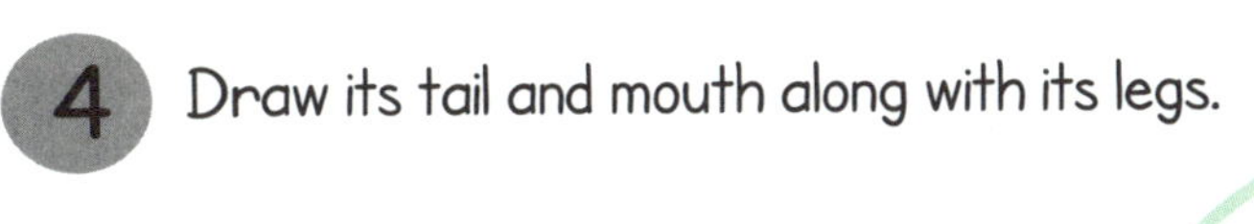

4 Draw its tail and mouth along with its legs.

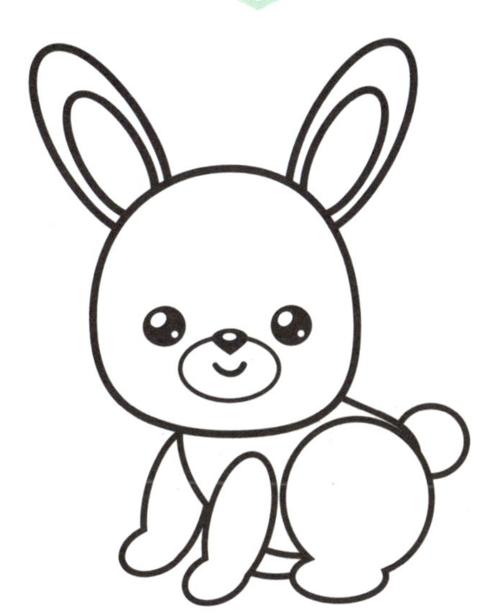

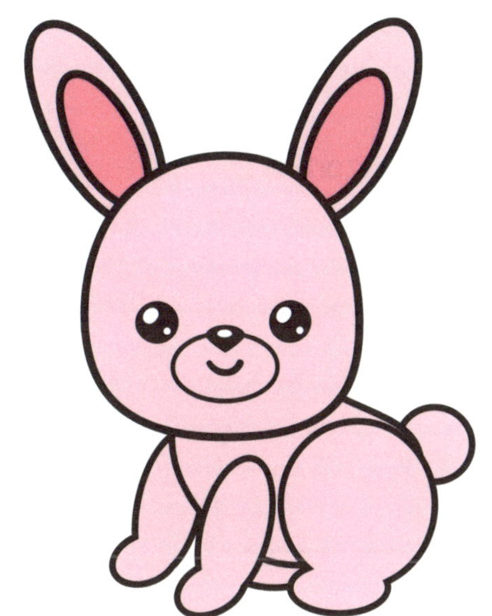

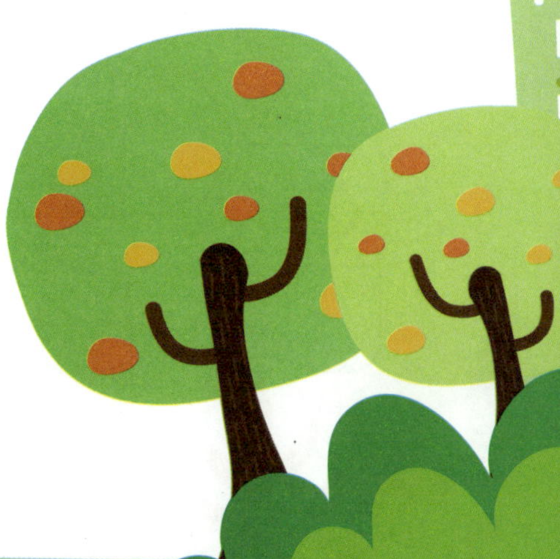

TORTOISE

A tortoise's shell is a natural armour that is its living fortress.

1 Draw a horizontal D.

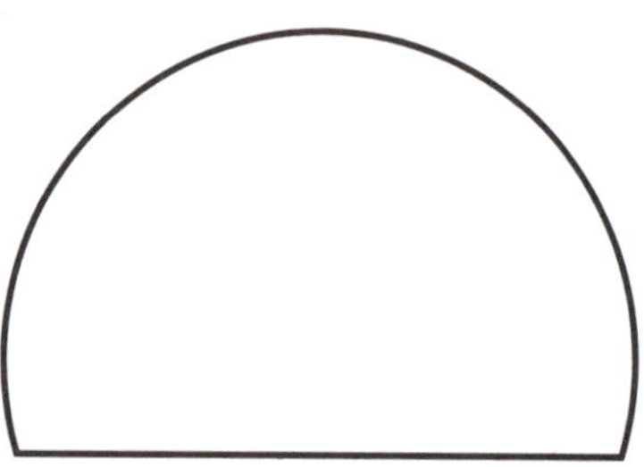

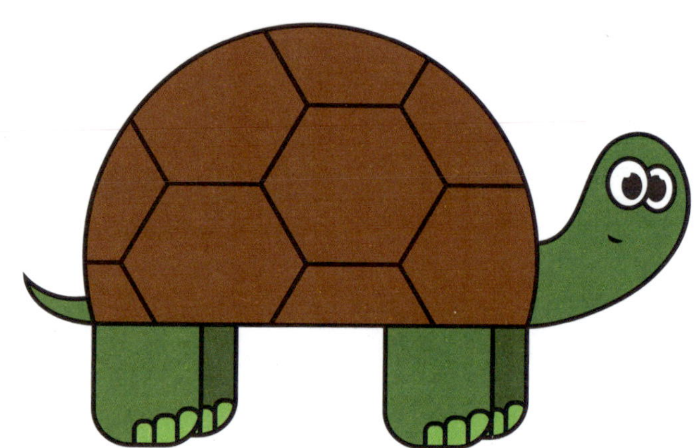

2 Draw the tortoise's tail, legs and face.

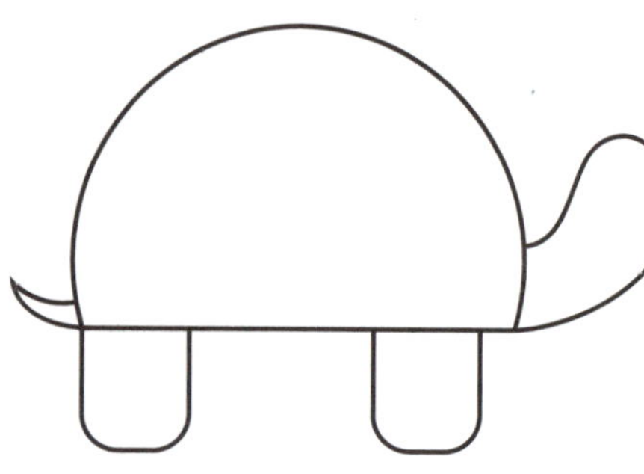

Draw Here

3 Draw details on its shell and legs. Draw its eyes, mouth and tail. Now, colour it as shown.

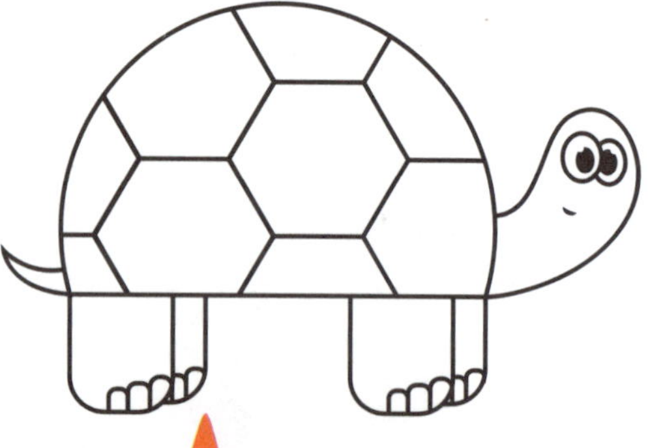

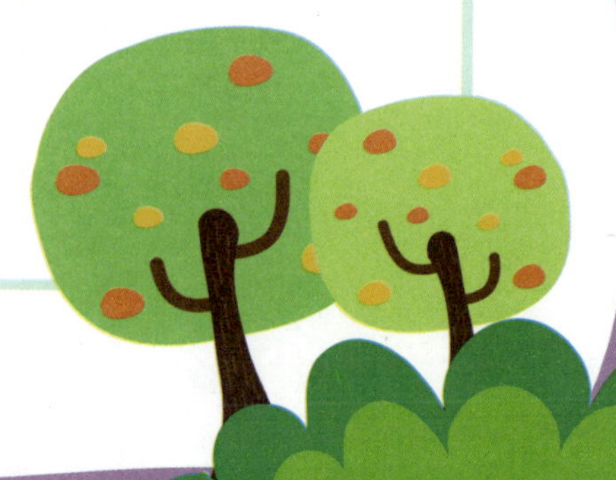